Dress and Popular Culture

Dress and Popular Culture

Edited by
Patricia A. Cunningham
and
Susan Voso Lab

Bowling Green State University Popular Press
Bowling Green, Ohio 43403

For our parents:

Clara Cunningham
Guy Clement Cunningham
Helen Joyce Hoke Voso and
Edward J. Voso

Contents

Introduction   1

Understanding Dress and Popular Culture   5
Patricia A. Cunningham and Susan Voso Lab

"We Girls Can Do Anything—Right Barbie!"
A Survey of Barbie Doll Fashions   19
Susan J. Dickey

American Denim: Blue Jeans
and Their Multiple Layers of Meaning   31
Beverly Gordon

Black Sororities and Fraternities:
A Case Study in Clothing Symbolism   46
Lillian O. Holloman

All Part of the Act:
A Hundred Years of Costume in
Anglo-American Popular Music   61
Albert LeBlanc

Punks   74
Barbara K. Nordquist

Paper Clothes:
Not Just a Fad   85
Alexandra Palmer

Senior Cords:
A Rite of Passage   106
Pamela J. Schlick and Kathleen L. Rowold

The Bicycle, the Bloomer
and Dress Reform in the 1890s   125
Sally Sims

Witches' Weeds   146
Pat Trautman

Contributors   156

Introduction

Clothing plays an important role in our lives. For it is often through its meaning that we substantiate our sense of self and our place in society. Clothing becomes, then, an indicator of our personal worth, values and beliefs as well as those of the culture in which we live. The associations that we have with dress have the potential to reveal the connections which we make with our culture in a very intimate way. Indeed, because clothing has multiple meanings and reflects our culture, it continues to capture the attention of scholars. Costume historians, anthropologists and social-psychologists strive to understand how clothes define individuals in time and place. We seek to capture the nuances of meaning through an understanding of how clothing functions in a culture. As scholars of material culture, we are ultimately concerned with seeking the meanings of things in people's lives. From the perspective of popular culture, the authors of these essays likewise seek answers to these questions about clothing, those most conspicuous objects of material popular culture.

The subjects of the essays range from looking at the ever changing meaning of specific garments and clothing practices of sub-cultural groups to examining dress as a reflection of changing life styles in American culture. The essays also embrace the subjects of fashion, fads and popular images. How we learn appropriate ways to dress and develop a vocabulary of dress-related meanings likewise are explored in the individual essays.

Dress, in the context of popular culture, includes clothing worn in everyday life, by ordinary people, as they go about the daily activities of their lives and carry on the traditions that bring meaning to them. We are concerned with how we use clothing to shape and define our identities, for we believe that our clothing expresses our individuality, personality and the sense we have of ourselves. Dress can reveal how we spend our working hours and leisure time. It reflects our gender, our occupations and group affiliations. Indeed, clothes are a measure of our very existence.

More specifically, the clothes of popular culture include the changing fashions and fads of the moment as well as more stable traditions, customs, and folkways of society. The dress of popular culture can be viewed as symbols which reflect political climate, technological patterns and economic conditions. Because clothes do all of these things, they have the potential to reveal a great deal about society. If we examine the clothing people wear for a variety of occasions and activities and analyze why they wear them and perhaps investigate how ideas about clothing are transmitted, then we may be able to understand how clothing relates to the changing patterns in technology, political trends, aesthetics and finally individual tastes and values.

We use clothing to communicate our individuality, and personality, our group and familial associations, our occupations and our status. We adorn our bodies in dress to fit into either the ideal standard for appropriate behavior or our own sense of aesthetics and beauty. We often expect others to be able to understand what we are communicating through these sartorial devices, and we in turn read the clothing messages sent by others. Indeed we share ideas about the meanings of these clothes, in a silent and ever changing vocabulary of meaning. But, what exactly is being said by our clothing? How are ideas transmitted about the meanings of dress, and what does this mean to scholars of popular American culture?

There are many texts on the history of dress that relate to us the fashions worn by the elite classes of past centuries, and likewise there are many books and journal articles that examine the social-psychology of clothing behavior. Such studies are extremely useful. From history we have gained a knowledge of what have been the prevailing styles of dress in different parts of the world over a long period of time. And through an examination of the social-psychology of dress a number of theories have been developed regarding the functions of clothing in society. By drawing on both the history of dress and the underlying assumptions presented in theoretical and scientific studies, we can examine popular usages of dress in society and gain perhaps a still greater understanding of how clothing functions and how ideas are transmitted to make the communication process so viable, and indeed, central to our lives.

Dress and Popular Culture hopes to shed new light on popular culture through a study of the associations of dress to culture. While journals and books in the disciplines of Social-psychology and Textiles and Clothing have focused on the meaning of dress, the literature of Popular Culture has included few entries on the subject. Yet in many respects clothing is perhaps one of the greatest barometers of popular culture in any period of time; it is, of course, always visible and ever changing with the times. The topics considered in this book seek to make up for this loss.

The first essay written by the editors addresses theories related to dress and popular culture. It provides the reader with a basis for understanding the meaning of dress in the context of popular culture.

Subsequent chapters illustrate the relationship between ideas reflected both in popular culture and clothing. In "We Girls Can Do Anything, Right Barbie!: A Case Study of Barbie Doll Fashions" Susan Dickey shows how the all-time favorite, the Barbie Doll, has become an icon of American culture, reflecting values and serving as a role model for young girls. Beverly Gordon reveals how a form of anti-fashion also can serve as identification for a group. Her essay, "American Denim: Blue Jeans and Their Multiple Layers of Meaning," also provides insight into how jeans went from work clothes to fashion, and ultimately became a symbol of America. Lillian Hollomans's essay, "Black Fraternities and Sororities: A Case Study of Clothing Symbolism," examines the ways in which groups use clothing in rites of passage, to distinguish themselves, and to create solidarity within a group. In "All Part of the Act: A Hundred Years of Costume in Anglo-American Popular Music," Al LeBlanc discusses how musicians create a persona or image through clothing. He examines the relationship between music style and clothing style, and investigates how musicians have been influenced by each other and the impact of their clothing styles on the public.

The clothing styles of the punks as discussed by Barbara K. Nordquist in her essay "Punks," likewise reveals the influence of music on fashion, particularly the sub-cultural style of the punks. In "Paper Dresses: Not Just a Fad," Alexandra Palmer examines fundamental truths behind the development of paper dresses, especially their integration with popular art and modern technology. Pam Schlick and Katherine Rowald discuss the use of a specific type of clothing for a rite of passage and social identification. Their essay, "Senior Cords: A Rite of Passage," shows how corduroy pants and skirts became a custom and part of Indiana youth culture, and its importance and use over a long period of time.

Sally Sims looks at the popularity of the bicycle for women in the 1890s. She examines the adoption of anti-fashionable clothing, the bloomer, as appropriate attire for that activity. Her essay, "The Bicycle, the Bloomer and Dress Reform," contributes to our knowledge of the impact of leisure activities on changing attitudes regarding women's dress as well as the power of fashion in denying women their new found freedom through dress. In "Witches Weeds," Pat Trautman discusses how we have come to recognize a witch. She examines the sources of our ideas regarding the stereotypical female witch that have become part of American popular culture and our image of the witch for Halloween and in children's literature.

As a barometer of popular culture, dress reflects cultural identity, values and symbols, as well as societal concepts of status, art and technology. As we begin pushing the boundaries of our discipline, in order to make linkages with other disciplines, we will find common ground upon which we all can explore and learn. The link between dress and popular culture offers us the opportunity to continue that search.

Understanding Dress and Popular Culture

Patricia A. Cunningham
and
Susan Voso Lab

Although readers of this book no doubt assume, as we do, that there is a relationship between clothing and popular culture, it may be wise to examine more closely some of the theories underlying the notion that clothing serves as a medium for the expression of popular culture. With this in mind, in this chapter we will discuss the concept of meaning in material objects, especially the communicative aspects of dress as sign and symbol. We will likewise focus on defining such concepts as culture, popular culture, clothing, fashion, fads, dress and identity, and antifashion. In this essay we will also address questions such as where does meaning come from, how is it conveyed and for whom? In doing so we will draw on examples from the essays included in this text.

Culture may be defined as the way of life, with shared abilities, habits, beliefs and customs of a people or social group. It is the entire complex of learned behaviors, transmitted to subsequent generations in an ever changing, cumulative, dynamic way (Horn and Gurel 36, Kaiser 277). Material objects, such as clothing, help to substantiate and give concrete cultural meaning to individuals. They are the media through which cultural ideas flow. That is, clothing helps to substantiate the manner in which we order our world of cultural categories such as class, status, gender and age, and express cultural principles such as the values, beliefs and ideas which we hold regarding our world (McCracken 73-77).

When we use the term popular culture, we are referring to that which belongs to the whole culture which shares common artifacts (Hall 55). Artifacts provide concrete evidence of past cultural beliefs and practices (Eydoux 3, xiii). Clothes, as artifacts, are important primary sources for scholarly investigation of earlier cultures (Hall 202). We define dress as mode or fashion of personal attire and costume (including style of hair, clothing and personal adornment) belonging to a particular nation, class or period. (Schevill 1). Evidence of what is popular in our culture is shown through the subjects of the essays in this book. The

Barbie Doll and her fashions, represent one of the most popular toys in history. The "Punk" look was a subculture trait which became fashion due to the wide acceptance and infusion into the culture. Denim apparel related to advertisements and the marketing process are also component parts of popular culture. Costume worn by popular musicians not only helped to create their persona, but also influenced public fashion choices. An early attempt at influencing women's apparel through the introduction of "bloomers" proved not to be popular, because societal pressure was too strong for this style to gain a foothold in fashion.

Meanings Communicated by Material Culture

We may call natural objects, or artifacts that are consumed or produced by a culture, material culture. These objects embody beliefs that may have been unexpressed because they are so fundamental or so universally understood in a particular culture. Artifacts, then, can be, as they were in the past, unconscious and unintentional conveyors of attitudes, values and beliefs. Artifacts are also intentional expressions of an aesthetic which is equal in meaning and importance to the unintentional expressions (Prown 79). While this belief is widely held regarding the symbolic nature of material objects, only recently have scholars developed theories and methods to pursue "how material culture achieves the outward expression of inward ideas" (McCracken 58).

As noted in Cordwell and Schwarz (28-31) clothes have long been ignored in studies of material culture. Yet as artifacts, they are associated with a complex of sentiments and serve to channel emotions; they move people to act in prescribed ways. Clothing can be empowered to express or conceal certain principles and emotions and move people to act in a culturally appropriate manner. This ability is evidence of its symbolic or rhetorical power to relate to action and commitment in a dynamic way. Indeed, according to Schwarz, more than any other material product, clothing plays a symbolic role in mediating the relationship between nature, people and their sociocultural environment (31).

In order to understand the social functions of costume we must learn to read them as signs in the same way we learn to read and understand languages (Bogatyrev 93). For clothes express the attitude of the wearer and therefore mirror the aesthetic, moral and nationalistic ideals of those who wear them. Clothing likewise expresses folk ethics (Bogatyrev 93). Indeed, when commenting on the importance of any goods or clothing, Grant McCracken observed that significance is found largely in their ability to carry and communicate meaning, rather than in their utilitarian and characteristic commercial value (71).

According to McCracken, the meaning of material objects travels from the cultural world to the object, and then from the object to individuals who, in the case of clothing, purchase them. In Western societies the transfer of meaning from the cultural world to commercial objects is facilitated by advertising and the fashion system. Meaning is transferred from the object to individuals through the mechanism of ritual, such as in the exchange of gifts, or in possession, grooming and divestment practices (McCracken 72).

The ideas and meanings associated with clothing may be transmitted visually or through written description. Either way, the garments convey their message through signs and symbols, and the meanings generated by clothing symbols relate directly to the function of clothing in a culture. The communicative function, however, may be different from language.

Although clothing does communicate, the use of the metaphor "clothing is a language," may not be accurate. According to McCracken, clothing does not function like language as a communicative system. For while the metaphor is popular with scholars and has pointed out the symbolic properties of material objects, it also has created misconceptions about what these properties are and how they operate (57). McCracken proposes, instead, a shift in the analysis to the examination of the differences between language and material culture. He suggests that we consider the following questions regarding the differences between material culture and language as expressive media: First, are material objects charged with meaning with which language is not entrusted? Second, does material culture work in more understated, inapparent ways than language? Are they less overt and less conscious than language? Third, do language and material culture differ in the universality of their codes? One disadvantage of material culture must be realized and that is the very limited range of its expressive capabilities. Objects cannot be combined, as words can, to generate new ideas. Perhaps the power of material culture lies in its instrumental function in constructing and ordering the self and the world (68). From this perspective, objects in our lives, and particularly clothing, are seen as essential to our identity in society.

We also look for meaning through the use of stereotypes. Stereotyping may be considered a shorthand and perhaps shortsighted means of using visual objects, or descriptions of objects, to communicate ideas. Stereotypes are simplified conventions or formulae which we develop and then repeat as a message in communication. The image immediately tells us what or who the person or object is. Thus, stereotyping relies on visual image, of which dress is an integral part, to relay a message (Hall 69, Horn and Gurel 161-62). Using clothing in this shorthand convention communicates a wide range of ideas in a manner that words cannot, more quickly, and to a wider audience.

In "Witches Weeds," Pat Trautman notes that our composite mental image of a witch's attire, a stereotypical witch, was created through literature rather than through the apparel actually worn by Salem women considered witches. "Her" dress and accessories were associated with causing specific harm to someone. The mass media, too, relies on the stereotype to convey the message of a witch, as in the movie "The Wizard of Oz" and in Walt Disney's "Snow White and the Seven Dwarfs." Since such films reach a wide audience, including all segments of the population, these ideas become generalized. The repeated use of the visual image of a witch perpetuates it as the stereotypical picture of a witch virtually unchanged over a long period of time.

The manner in which clothing communicates, as in stereotypes, can also be explained in terms of symbolic interaction theory (Horn and Gurel 158-60, Kaiser 184-5) developed by George Herbert Mead. This theory states that we respond to clothing symbols on the basis of the meanings they have for us. For communication to occur, the meanings must be shared by the wearer and the viewer (Kaiser 185). The information that is communicated is then directly related to the function or purposes of the clothing as shared by the interactors. In our culture these purposes cover a wide range of activities. As spelled out by Roach and Eicher (121-38), clothing reflects individual or group identity (such as gender, social role, occupational role, economic status, political belief or allegiances), or identifies cultural ritual and rites of passage (such as marriage or religious beliefs and entertainments) shared by members of society. In "Senior Cords" Schlick and Rowold point out that the wearing of special corduroy trousers or skirts was taken seriously by participating seniors, and that they symbolized, in a very public way, the passage into the adult world from 1912 to 1972. In her essay on black sororities, Holloman used the example of pledging and associated rites of intensification (rituals marking an occasion) to indicate a change in role and status for the individual within the organization (sorority) and also to nonsorority members.

Appropriate Dress and Identity

While theoretical development regarding the expressive power of dress is fairly recent, clothing images have long been used by artists to communicate ideas in the visual arts. Indeed, the associative power of dress was apparent in the early art theorists such as Leon Battista Alberti, Lodovico Dolce, André Félebien, Roger DePiles and the eighteenth-century English painter William Hogarth. They recognized "the importance of costume in depicting decorum, or what is fitting and agreeable to an occasion or person in a painting." They believed that the character of individuals, their age, sex, rank, status and country of origin, could be achieved through careful attention to dress (Cunningham 51-4).

In the eighteenth century visual objects were thought to have great persuasive powers. Indeed, Hogarth stated that "ocular demonstration will convince and improve man sooner than ten thousand fols" (215). In the *Analysis of Beauty*, Hogarth stated that "fitness is first considered by them [women] as knowing that their dresses should be useful, commodious, and fitted to their different ages; or rich, airy, and loose, agreeable to the character they would give out to the public by their dress" (20).

Hogarth not only believed in the importance of appropriate dress in a painting to achieve didactic ends, but he drew on dress to illustrate his six principles of beauty and related aesthetic concepts in his *Analysis of Beauty*. His statements on dress suggest that he was well acquainted with the psychological and social functions of clothing in society, for he dealt directly with ideas regarding modesty, adornment, role, status and characterization.

Appropriate dress is no more essential in a painting than it is in life. For dress in paintings reflects culture, that is, it reflects the way we, as social creatures, use dress to define our place in society. As society became more complex, in the nineteenth century, specific clothing came to be associated with various societal categories such as those designated by McCracken—time, space and the human categories of class, status, gender, age, and occupation (73). Indeed, an involved ritual of wearing specific clothes for different occasions, events, times of day and rites of passage soon emerged. As ideas of appropriate clothing became intertwined with rules of acceptable behavior, specific types of clothing became synonymous with correct behavior. Judgment would then be made according to the principles or values of the culture.

Studies in human behavior indicate that, regardless of the size of the group or society in which membership is thought to be important, there is a need on the part of the individual to belong, to fit in, and to be accepted by the rest of the "group" or society. One way to show acceptance of the group's philosophy and standards is to dress in a way that reflects those same ideals. Society has expectations or notions of what is acceptable attire for those who are socially mature (Roach and Eicher 44, 83). In the socialization process people learn about appropriate dress, and then use this knowledge to help themselves fit comfortably into society. One example of this concept may be seen in the packaging and sales of the "Dress-for-Success" Barbie Doll. In her essay on "Barbie," Susan Dickey describes how the ideal forms of appropriate dress were presented in "toy" form. Barbie, representing the grown-up world, exemplified American ideals of glamour and affluence. The ideas of wearing the "right" clothes provided high degrees of happiness, self-worth and status. In her study of black sororities, Holloman also reveals the importance of clothing to sorority members who rely on outward symbols which reflect the standards and ideals of each organization.

In our culture we identify individuals, groups or subgroups and their related characteristics through the clothing symbols associated with them. Examples of apparel indicating group membership may be found in the essays on black sororities and senior cords. Clothing symbols may, however, change in meaning over time. For instance, the Bloomer, a cycling garment, symbolized the "wheelwoman" of the 1890s. In the 1850s that same garment was a symbol of the "radical" suffragist. The Bloomer, in its day, no doubt sparked a sense of rebellion among its wearers. Today that rebellion may be sensed in the lifestyle and associated dress of *Punks*.

An excellent example of the evolving associations given to dress can be found in the study of denim apparel by Beverly Gordon. Denim, in early history, reminds us of a rugged male Westerner or if worn by a female, visions of early "tomboys." As time passed one segment of society may have seen denim relating to naturalists, artists or bohemians, while others viewed denim apparel as a statement against "the establishment" or the Vietnam War. Denim in later years also symbolized high status seekers and eventually a generally accepted American "uniform." When we compare the band uniforms in past history to current popular music apparel, we identify not only specific groups, but also the particular responsibilities of individuals within that group through an examination of their fashions, grooming and accessories.

Mass Fashion: A Reflection of Culture

Historically, folk societies have been replaced by mass culture and mass behavior. Today, societies are mass societies made up of concentrations of large numbers of people in large metropolitan areas, characteristically post industrial, and participating in mass activity: producing, marketing and consuming large volumes of materials (Roach and Eicher 185, Kaiser 403). Urban settings, industrialization, and the development of mass transportation and communication systems also directly affected fashion. Clothing styles, once unique and handcrafted, became more simple (Kaiser 397, 403). Fashions in mass society became mass fashion with traditional apparel giving way to automation, resulting in commercially produced clothing consumed in large quantities (Schevill, 4). Mass fashion reflects the many and complex cultural changes occurring in society including the influences of technology, government, and mass communication.

Technological advancements eventually resulted in a high degree of automation with an emphasis upon modernization, high volume and rapid change in our culture and our fashions. As early technological advances entered the cultural mainstream, they became infused into consumer goods, such as fashion. For example, the invention of the bicycle directly influenced and helped to bring about dress reform. In "The Bicycle, the Bloomer and Dress Reform in the 1890s" Sally Sims points out that bicycling promoted the use of flexible corsets, a rear wheel dress guard and shortened skirt lengths. The bicycle proved to be a catalyst to improving women's clothing for specific activities outside the home, in the workplace and during foul weather.

A direct influence of modern technology on apparel may be seen through the invention of paper clothes. Alexander Palmer reveals that new nonwoven textile technologies were incorporated into the production of paper products which were, in turn, made into dresses and other apparel items. Paper clothing reflected the most recent technologies and provided us with a futuristic view of apparel.

The age of electric sound, vibrating colors, and intense, fast paced and demanding lifestyles may be measured through the wardrobes of today's popular musicians. The newly developed stretch fabrics, metallic yarns, day-glow dyes, and plastic glittering sequins worn by performers helps them capture our attention. According to Al LeBlanc, the use of such attention-getting apparel helps to promote the popular musician.

Fashion also reflects the collective behavior of mass culture. Styles are influenced by social and political values. Fashion is today a democratic process where individual consumers, through their marketplace voting, direct the course of popular styles. Dress represents personal choice (Kaiser 360, 388-9, 406). In exercising the right to choose from the mass of available styles our democratic ideas are reflected. Paper dress and denim attire were affordable by the masses, offered newness and change, and proved to be both functional and futuristic. A philosophy of innovation and change is as much a part of the American culture as it is in our fashions (Kaiser, 404).

Mass communication, which transmits the fashion message to large numbers of people, helps to promote fashion change (Kaiser 403). Not only is change in fashion communicated, but as a part of planned obsolescence, this idea for change becomes desirable. Feeling the need to replace last year's fashions for the upcoming season is the primary goal of the fashion industry.

Being able to maintain a fashionable appearance has some influence on our self-concept. The concept of self refers to a stable, all encompassing idea of who we are, based on information received through socialization, self-expression and identity (Kaiser 59). We have some indication of who we are from the sum of all our past experiences, interactions, and feedback from others (Kaiser 93, 199). Clothing helps to define our identity by supplying cues and symbols that assist us in categorizing within the culture. Status symbols serve to identify or socially "place" an individual (Kaiser 387). Status refers to a person's position in a social hierarchy

(Kaiser 364). Making a distinction about status through dress is shown in a number of this book's essays. Popular musician's apparel is essentially celebrity status attire. Barbie has been dressed to look successful, and even yuppie to raise her status. Social success was achieved because paper clothing offered a highly modern appearance. Denim apparel at one time symbolized high status seekers when expensive designer labels were added.

As change in an individual's status occurs this, too, is indicated through dress. Rites of intensification, causing changes in status, may occur at specific times in a person's life. In an evaluation of the significance of senior cords, Schlick and Rowald surmised that this garment was a public declaration by all participating Indiana high school seniors which symbolized passage into the adult world. Those who participated in wearing senior cords considered this a serious activity. Just as serious, Holloman notes that black sorority members wore distinctive clothing symbols during various stages of the initiation process. The clothing symbols directly related to the ritual were shared by each sorority member.

For clothing symbols to be meaningful, they do not have to indicate status. The symbols associated with the attire of the witch or witches weeds have carried meaning through centuries of time. According to Pat Trautman, the first women accused of being witches wore outmoded fashions which indicated economic rather than social status. Later, through literary depictions rather than the actual clothing, witches were identified through symbols associated with bewitching capabilities (brooms, black cats, yellowbirds) and apparel "designed" by promoters of Halloween and by Disney stories and movies.

Dress also symbolizes changes in societal values and attitudes. As Alexander Palmer indicates in her discussion of paper clothes, society was making a statement for change. Paper clothing supported the desire for a portable lifestyle that could be discarded and replaced at our convenience for little money. This throw-away concept reflected a more casual or liberated attitude toward sex, relationships, or permanency.

In Western societies mass fashion, through its symbols, functions in a culturally revealing and meaningful way, for fashionable goods are the bearers of cultural meaning. Fashion therefore is an important force in maintaining and preserving the values of culture, and in reflecting changes in society as well.

The Function of Mass Fashion in Communicating Cultural Meaning
According to Grant McCracken, cultural meaning is transferred from the cultural world to goods which we purchase and use in everyday life. As objects of popular culture, clothing carries considerable cultural meaning which is in a constant state of evolution and change. Advertising

aids in the transmission of meaning from the culturally constituted world to consumer goods. But more important for our study is McCracken's analysis of the fashion system as an instrument in the transfer of meaning. In the fashion system, goods are constantly being invested and divested of meaningful properties in three ways. First, as in advertising, through photography in magazines or newspapers, efforts are made to conjoin the world and goods, where the visual glimpse of the idea from the cultural world (categories and principles) placed in proximity to a worldly good (clothing), creates a connection that is not lost on the consumer. Meaning then moves from the culturally constituted world to the object (79).

Second, the fashion system invents new cultural meanings through opinion leaders who help shape and define cultural meaning. Opinion leaders are individuals held in high esteem (movie stars, celebrities, nobility, etc.). Their behavior is emulated by those who admire them. In a third capacity, the fashion system engages in a more radical reform which is generated by those subcultures on the fringes of society (punks, gays, hippies, etc.). These groups deviate readily from the norms of society because they are not really part of it. Society simply tolerates these aberrations and, indeed, in a peculiar way, accepts the new meaning of cultural categories created by these groups. These ideas thus enter the cultural mainstream and are often adopted for mass fashion. The agents who gather up these meanings to translate them into goods are first, the designers of products, and second, fashion journalists, social observers and market researchers (McCracken 79-83). Thanks to advertising and the fashion system, objects carry a variety of meanings in a culture. The meaning of these goods then must be transferred to the consumer. According to McCracken this is carried out through a system of rituals by individuals (83-4).

The meaning of clothing, particularly the style of clothing can be communicated outside of the fashion system as well. And this is certainly true of subcultural dress and anti-fashion as expressed through two examples presented in this group of essays, "Punks" and "The Bicycle, the Bloomer and Dress Reform in the 1890s."

Anti-fashion

Anti-fashion is any style in clothing which goes against what is currently in fashion. It is viewed as a means of making a political statement, and is meant to communicate a message about the group that embraces it. It often reflects beliefs, attitudes and ideas of subcultures of the larger culture. The dress functions as a sign of rejection of the norm and hence the status quo, as well as an adherence to thought and ideas of the fringe of society. Anti-fashion can be rebellious in nature and make a statement through its style that clearly says no to the hegemony of the prevailing style of fashion. The clothing is immediately perceived as a particular style and the person wearing the clothes as a particular type who transmits beliefs through the medium of clothing (Hebdige 17).

Because anti-fashion becomes a sign of a subculture, it is therefore part of popular culture and may, indeed, involve large segments of the population at any given time. While anti-fashion is a style that reflects subculture, it also can be viewed as a style of dress which is associated with an issue, not necessarily a single group. That is, it may reflect an idea which crosses paths with different groups, even different economic and social classes. The subcultural type is represented by the punks; issue oriented anti-fashion is exemplified by the dress reform movement of the nineteenth century.

Punk Style

In punk style "anything within and without reason could be turned into part of what Vivian Westwood called 'confrontation dressing' so long as the rupture between 'natural' and constructed context was clearly visible" (Hebdige 107). For it was important to communicate both difference and an identity denoted by a style that is revealed through its own distinctive rituals of consumption. With the punks, the most unremarkable and inappropriate items could be brought within the province of style. As noted by Hebdige:

Objects borrowed from the most sordid of contexts found a place in the punks' ensembles: lavatory chains were draped in graceful arcs across chests encased in plastic bin-liners. Safety pins were taken out of their domestic 'utility' context and worn as gruesome ornaments through the cheek, ear or lip. 'Cheap' trashy fabrics (PVC, plastic, lurex, etc.) in vulgar designs (eg., mock leopard skin) and 'nasty' colours, long discarded by the quality end of the fashion industry as obsolete kitsch, were salvaged by the punks and turned into garments (fly boy drainpipes, 'common' miniskirts) which offered self-conscious commentaries on the notions of modernity and taste... Hair was obviously dyed (hay yellow, jet black, or bright orange with tufts of green or bleached in question marks), and T-shirts and trousers told the story of their own construction with multiple zips and outside seams clearly displayed. (107)

Of course the punks upset other traditional aspects of culture as well. Dance and music and ultimately the fashionable world itself were influenced or transformed by its style. Dancing, a usually expressive medium in British rock and mainstream pop culture was turned into a dumb show of blank robotics (Hebdige 108). And music too was similarly distinguished from the normal popular and rock forms. Regarding harmonics, "they were into chaos, not music" (Hebdige 109). It was, precisely in the performance arena that punk groups posed the clearest threat to law and order. Certainly, they succeeded in subverting the conventions of concert and nightclub entertainment. Most significantly, they attempted both physically and in terms of lyrics and life-style to move closer to their audiences. This in itself is by no means unique: the boundary between artist and audience has often stood as a metaphor in revolutionary aesthetics (Brecht, the surrealists, Dada, Marcuse, etc.) for that larger and more intransigent barrier which separates art and the dream from reality and life under capitalism. The stages of those venues secure enough to host 'new wave' acts were regularly invaded by hordes of punks, and if the management refused to tolerate such blatant disregard for ballroom etiquette, then the groups and their followers could be drawn closer together in a communion of spittle and mutual abuse.(Hebdige 110)

As Al LeBlanc observes in "All Part of the Act," the punk persona on stage helped to transmit the style to the public. When popularized through the media of both music and dance, the punk style became popular with youth in America who embraced the style as an expression of rebelliousness and a reflection of independence. As Nordquist notes in her essay, "Punks," clothing designers used the style to give energy to new creations. Real punks embraced the style to reflect their alienation and feelings of separation and rejection from the larger society. It is clear, then, that not all punks were equally committed to the style:

Different youths bring different degrees of commitment to a subculture. It can represent a major dimension in people's lives—an axis erected in the face of the family around which a secret and immaculate identity can be made to cohere—or it can be a slight distraction, a bit of light relief from the monotonous but none the less paramount realities of school, home and work. It can be used as a means of escape, of total detachment from the surrounding terrain, or as a way of fitting back in to it and settling down after a week-end or evening spent letting off steam.(Hebdige 122)

Regardless of the degree of commitment to the punk subculture, all members shared a common language:

The subculture was nothing if not consistent. There was a homological relation between the trashy cut-up clothes and spiky hair, the pogo and amphetamines, the spitting, the vomiting, the format of the fanzines, the insurrectionary poses and the 'soulless', frantically driven music. The punks wore clothes which were the sartorial equivalent of swear words, and they swore as they dressed—with calculated effect, lacing obscenities into record notes and publicity releases, interviews and love songs. (Hebdige 122)

Dress Reform
While they seem mildly eccentric compared to the punks, the dress reformers of the nineteenth century were also engaging in a form of anti-fashion when they adopted bloomers and other styles of dress that did not conform to current fashion or standards of acceptable dress. They believed that the position of women in society was clearly reflected in

their dress. The tight corsets and long, heavy skirts restricted movement, they were unhealthy and clearly were symbols of oppression as well. In the second half century these advocates of rational dress included feminists who supported suffrage and temperance like Elizabeth Cady Stanton, Amelia Bloomer and Francis Willard, as well as reformers in education, health, physical culture, dance and art.

Since these individuals and groups seeking reform had diverse interests, it is not surprising that they sought somewhat different solutions to the problem. The initial reformers at mid century chose the "Bloomer Costume," a short dress and full cut trousers gathered at the ankle, which took its name from the editor of *The Lily*, Amelia Bloomer. Still others chose to reform undergarments. They developed systems of underclothes that reduced the number of undergarments worn and removed stays from corsets. They developed one-piece undergarments (union suits) which also reduced bulk. Others chose more artistic rational dress based on aesthetic principles. These artistic dresses, adaptations of historic styles (especially medieval or classical Greek dress) or styles similar to current fashions, were altered to be comfortable and were usually worn over one of the rational systems of undergarments.

The clothing worn for bicycling may have developed from the "Bloomer Costume," or from clothing worn for gymnastics and other physical activities that women were beginning to enjoy such as hiking, swimming and physical culture. By the 1860s the "Bloomer Costume" had lost favor with many feminists because they felt that it detracted from their cause when worn in public. However, the Bloomer remained a symbol of women's oppression. And it continued to be worn in more private settings for gymnastics and sports.

In the 1890s, a form of Bloomer was revived by the Dress Reform Committee of the National Council of Women. They suggested three acceptable variations: the gymnasium suit, a Syrian costume and a business dress, the American costume. The National Council then recommended that women wear a version of these reform garments to the Columbian Exposition in 1893 (Russell 76). While the acceptance of these garments in the 1890s by the National Council of Women may have been owing to their suitability and acceptance for leisure activities, they were nonetheless still making a political statement about women's health and the need for reform.

As Sally Sims notes in "The Bicycle, the Bloomer and Dress Reform in the 1890s," after the middle of the decade women ceased to wear the Bloomer and chose instead a shortened skirt for bicycle riding. The sight of women wearing trousers in public was no doubt still unacceptable to many Americans. It was only in private that Bloomers were acceptable dress. Yet by the 1890s women were engaging more and more in both private and public sports and activities where Bloomer styles were expected. The freedom of movement allowed by the clothing was suited to the rigor of the sport. However, acceptance of sports clothes occurred only within the confines of the activity. When women's sports became more rigorous, the clothing was altered to allow more movement, but this did not occur in the public sphere until well into the twentieth century.

Conclusion

We recognize the powerful communicative aspect of dress. It can express consciously or unconsciously our personal attitudes, values, beliefs and emotions and in turn those aspects of the larger culture. Whether we draw on stereotypes to know a person or reflect on the clothing in a painting, we often "know" a person through their dress.

We learn meanings associated with clothing from customary use in a society. Through associations made in print and visual media objects are invested with meaning. And it is from these learned shared ideas that we communicate through dress.

The idea of appropriateness in dress is important for both expressions of self and to show group affiliation. The rules of propriety control what we wear today. We need to appear "right" in order to conform to groups to which we belong or those in which we seek membership. The group may represent our occupation or it may reflect identification with a subculture such as the punks.

Clothes that reflect popular culture can be read in light of the meaning invested in them. Dress provides a way then, to explore culture on an intimate plane which taps into individual thoughts, hopes and dreams, as well as general ideas, attitudes and beliefs of the masses. Scholars of material culture may find a treasure trove of learning in the threads and thoughts that have woven our dress and created our culture.

Works Cited

Bogatyrev, Peter. *Functions of Folk Costume in Moravian Slovakia.* Trans. Richard G. Crum. The Hague: Mouton, 1971.

Cordwell, J.M. and Schwarz, R.A. *The Fabrics of Culture: The Anthropology of Clothing and Adornment.* The Hague: Mouton, 1979.

Cunningham, Patricia A. "The Theoretical Bases of William Hogarth's Depictions of Dress." *Dress. The Annual Journal of the Costume Society of America* 7 (1981): 52-68.

Eydoux, Henri-Paul. *The Buried Past.* New York: Frederick A. Praeger, 1966.

Hall, Stuart and Whannel, Paddy. *The Popular Arts.* Boston: Beacon, 1964.

Hebdige, Dick. *Subculture. The Meaning of Style.* London: Methuen, 1979.

Hogarth, William. *The Analysis of Beauty.* Ed. Joseph Burke. Oxford: Clarendon, 1955.

Horn, M.J. and Gurel, L.M. *The Second Skin*. Boston: Houghton-Mifflin, 1981.

Kaiser, Susan. *The Social Psychology of Clothing*. New York: MacMillan, 1985.

McCracken, Grant. *Culture and Consumption*. Bloomington, IN: Indiana UP, 1988.

Prown, Jules D. et al. "Material Culture Studies: A Symposium."*Material Culture* 17 (1985): 77-114.

Roach, M.E. and Eicher, J.B. *The Visible Self: Perspectives on Dress*. Englewood Cliffs, NJ: Prentice-Hall, 1973.

Russell, Frances. E. "Freedom in Dress for Women." *Arena* 8 (1893):71-7.

Schevill, Margot Blum. *Costume as Communication*. Bristol, RI: Haffenreffer Museum of Anthropology, 1986.

"We Girls Can Do Anything—Right Barbie!"
A Survey of Barbie Doll Fashions

Susan J. Dickey

Barbie, the 11 1/2 inch fashion doll from Mattel Toys, Inc., is one of the most popular toys in history. Since her introduction in 1959 over 200 million dolls, including family and friends like sister Skipper and boyfriend Ken, have been sold (*Barbie Through the Years* 1). The phenomenal success and longevity, practically unheard of in the toy industry, makes Barbie one of the hottest American popular culture items of the twentieth century. The product's endurance is due primarily to its intrinsic play value. With imagination, as well as hands, a child can use the doll in many ways; it becomes whatever she wants. The numerous accouterments, such as houses, automobiles, and pets, have play value as well. These "props" also encourage additional consumer purchase to enlarge Barbie's world.

The Barbie doll fashions, more than any other aspect of play value, have contributed to the doll's mass appeal. Based on *haute couture* and American sportswear prototypes, the clothing, including shoes and accessories, is an integral part of the Barbie persona. Girls, as well as mothers and collectors, find vicarious pleasure in Barbie's luxurious gowns. In real life, people can purchase fashionable sportswear in discount stores, but fanciful costumes are beyond the purse of most Americans whose lifestyles offer no occasions to wear stunning evening dresses. Barbie, however, can attend any number of black tie events in an afternoon of play.

How Barbie dolls and the fashions reflect American ideals of glamour and affluence is the subject of this discourse. But is the Barbie doll more than a symbol? Is it a role model with lasting effects for the girls who play with the doll? These questions will be addressed through a brief survey of the product; a review of typical play situations such as dating, fashion modeling, wedding and career fantasies; and results of a questionnaire on the doll conducted by the author in 1987.

The questionnaire was written and funded by the author. It was distributed through a network of friends and colleagues. Respondents were women age 18 and over who had played with the Barbie doll as children. The purpose of the questionnaire was to assess attitudes and beliefs about the doll, as well as to gather quanitative information. Of 150 questionnaires distributed 74, or approximately 50 percent, were returned.

A majority of respondents, fifty-eight percent, indicated that the clothing items and playing with them were their favorite aspects of Barbie play (Barbie questionnaire). Many of those who answered the questionnaire were clothing and textile students and professionals, and therefore, might be expected to have an unusually high interest in the fashions, but their appeal seemed to cut across lines of age and occupation. Most of the 88 lenders to the Indiana State Museum's 1984 exhibition, "25 Years of Barbie Dolls," also cited the fashions as the most appealing aspect of Barbie play. The lenders, mostly women in their twenties and early thirties, represented a broad spectrum of interests, careers, and educational levels.

Affordability of the fashions has also been a factor in Barbie's popularity. In 1986, for example, a fancy and versatile gown from the Oscar de la Renta series cost about $10 (Fig. 1), but a furnished Dream House ran about $100. Consistently, the fashions have offered a great deal of play value for the money.

Surprisingly, Mattel did not seem to realize the vast marketing potential of the fashions until the 1970s. Until then most Barbie dolls came in a swimsuit and all other costumes were sold separately. The Live Action dolls of 1971, dressed in fringed rock and roll outfits, were among the first in which the apparel could be obtained only by purchasing the doll. Today that practice is standard, thus increasing Barbie's baseline price and prompting girls to ask for additional dolls.

Early on, critics alleged that Barbie over-emphasized beauty, fashionable dress, and the acquisition of material things. In 1964 *The Nation* stated, "...she is a Machiavellian do-gooder, a social climber and a tedious narcissist. Her favorite sports are tennis, skiing and dressing herself." Two years later Chauncey Howell lambasted Barbie's plastic sexuality and preoccupation with fashion in *Women's Wear Daily*. Similar comments appeared in *Ms.* over a decade later: "The Barbie doll is a stereotype made flesh. Well, vinyl, anyway." (Leavy).

Mattel has claimed that Barbie was never intended to be a role model for girls (Irving). But like all dolls, Barbie replicates the human body and, therefore, human characteristics are projected onto it. With vital statistics of 5 1/2-3-5 inches the doll's gender is obviously female and feminine word forms are almost always used when describing Barbie.

Ironically, her full bosom was out of fashion until recently. Barbie's figure was sculpted after ideals of the 1950s. She managed to embody the sex appeal and glamor of Bridgitte Bardot, Marilyn Monroe, and Kim Novak with the wholesomeness of Doris Day. According to fashion designer and Barbie doll collector Billy Boy, Barbie is based on Lille, a German doll that in turn was taken from a cartoon by Reinhard Beuthien. Lille's success was short lived and the rights were sold to Mattel (Billy Boy 19).

Ruth Handler, one of Mattel's co-founders, was responsible for the American Barbie. Handler observed that her daughter Barbara enjoyed playing with teen-age paper dolls, their fashions, and accessories. Thus, the Barbie doll was conceived as a three dimensional "teen-age fashion model" and named in honor of Handler's daughter (DeWein, Ashabraner 1). The Barbie doll was clothed in exquisite *haute couture* apparel and the best of American sportswear. The golden age of Barbie thus began.

Mattel designers were inspired by Paris originals for many of the evening gowns, party dresses, and day suits in the line. "After 5" and "Enchanted Evening" showed the influence of Dior (Fig. 1) as did "Saturday Matinee," a particularly stylish brown wool and Lurex suit (Fig. 2). One saw hints of Balenciaga in "Career Girl" (Fig. 4). A well-trained eye could detect traces of Schiaparelli, Chanel, and other *couturiers* (Billy Boy 22-5, 35). Barbie looked as if she had stepped from the pages of *Vogue* or *Harper's Bazaar* in many of the 150 ensembles produced from 1959 to 1966.

Fig. 1 (from left) After 5, Enchanted Evening, Oscar de la Renta Collector Series IX.

Fig. 2 (from left) Friday Nite Date, Campus Sweetheart, Senior Prom, Saturday Matinee.

Fig. 3 (from left) Tennis Anyone, Winter Holiday, Ski Queen.

Girls playing with the doll were unaware of the wardrobe's lofty origins, but they recognized similar styles in their mothers' closets. Girls also understood that the decolleté gowns and skin tight pants, like Barbie herself, represented the world of grown-ups, a world they were preparing to enter. Suzanne Alexander received a Barbie doll on her thirteenth birthday in the early sixties. Some years later as a lender to the Indiana exhibition she wrote:

I was just getting interested in clothes, make-up and the "idea" of going on dates to school dances. At that time, Barbie and her friend Midge...represented to me the "model" teen-agers, ones right out of *Seventeen* magazine. I could dress them in fantasy clothes (ones I wished I could own and wear) and send them off to dozens of proms.

Dating was a major activity for Barbie. Seventy-nine percent of questionnaire respondents sometimes pretended Barbie dated. The Ken doll, Barbie's boyfriend, debuted in 1961, but even girls without Ken acted out dating fantasies; imagination was everything.

For a price, usually $1.50 to $3.50, Mattel provided a plethora of outfits suitable for dates. In fact, six Barbie fashions incorporated the word into their titles. They were "Friday Nite Date" (Fig. 2), "Movie Date," "Party Date," "Theatre Date," "Lunch Date", and "Disco Date." Other titles such as "Saturday Matinee," "Campus Sweetheart," and "Senior Prom" (Fig. 2) implied a dating situation. Ken had an assortment of tuxedos, dress suits, and casual attire so he could properly escort Barbie to those and numerous other events alluded to in costume titles like "Country Club Dance," "Fraternity Dance," "Debutante Party," "Lunch on the Terrace," and "Outdoor Art Show." "Tennis Anyone," "Winter Holiday," and "Ski Queen" (Fig. 3) and other sportswear provided dating possibilities as well.

Pretend weddings were nearly as widespread as dates. Nearly all of the exhibition lenders and 57% of questionnaire respondents created wedding fantasies. Lender Kristina Payne recalled that her dolls dated until she could save enough allowance to buy the genuine Mattel Barbie wedding dress, a costly investment of $5.00. Liz Kehlbeck, another lender recalled:

The highlight of one summer...was the "Barbie Wedding!" My sister designed invitations, we drew a wedding cake (it was scaled for Barbie), took pictures, Midge was maid of honor, [Barbie] married Ken of course.

If bored with weddings, Barbie could always painlessly revert to the single life and many imagined her to be a working woman with her own car and home. An anonymous lender wrote:

In pretend situations, Barbie was usually single and lived in an apartment with her friend or sister...I can't really say why I never played that she was married. I had a Ken doll, but I think it had something to do with the move toward female independence (feminist movement, if you will) or maybe my own desire for independence.(Anonymous 1)

All the costumes might be said to represent a career in modeling, but at least 11 ensembles depicted specific jobs or professions, most of them traditionally held by females. That occupations, other than nursing, were shown at all was a breakthrough in the doll world. "Candy Striper Volunteer," (Fig. 4), "Student Teacher," "Registered Nurse," "American Airlines Stewardess," and "Pan American Airways Stewardess" exemplified jobs typical of girls' career aspirations in the early sixties.

Then, as now, many little girls dreamed of becoming ballet dancers. One version of today's My First Barbie is a ballerina, but in the golden age the separately purchased ballerina costume (Fig. 4) came with practice leotard and tights, toe shoes, and a satin tote.

Because Barbie's official persona was that of a teen-age fashion model, it was not surprising that some ensembles portrayed fashion careers, another path open to females at the time. "Busy Gal" (Fig. 4) was a red silk suit accessorized with a portfolio containing two fashion illustrations. "Junior Designer" came with a miniature iron and "Fashion Editor" had a camera.

"Commuter Set" was more general in character, a good all-purpose black knit suit (Fig. 4). The hat box suggested that Barbie's profession might be shopping, but the suit did have play value as did "Career Girl" (Fig. 4).

"Career Girl," a salt and pepper tweed suit with red sweater was the most versatile of vocational ensembles. It looked like something Ann Sothern might have worn on television in her role as business woman Katie O'Connor.

The golden age came to a close in the early 1970s. Barbie's Mod fashions of the late sixties maintained high standards of design and construction, but by 1973 zippers and buttons had been replaced by snaps and ties. Fine cottons, woolens, silks, and quality synthetics gave way to inferior grades of fabric.

Except for examples held by collectors, the Barbie dolls themselves used after the mid-sixties did not hold up well. Wear and grime characterize these dolls in part because the age of first Barbie play had declined from about seven to about five. Another reason was mechanical innovations in the doll bodies that did little to enhance play value, but added parts that frequently broke. Most of the so-called improvements, such as jointed thumbs, "living" hip joints, and "natural action" torsos, were dropped by 1980.

Fig. 4 (from left) Career Girl, Ballerina, Candy Striper Volunteer, Commuter Set, Busy Gal.

The Barbie doll of 1967 had a new face and the patented Twist'N Turn waist. She was younger and more innocent looking than her predecessor. Costume titles like "The Yellow Go," "Zokka!," "Movie Groovie," "Fab City," and "Leisure Leopard" no longer hinted at play paths, but mirrored the relaxed moral standards and sense of fun that prevaded the youth culture. No more stuffy titles such as "Debutante Party" for Barbie. After all, ladies—now called women—no longer wore gloves and hats for everyday outings or even formal occasions.

A doctor and United Airlines Stewardess outfits were the only occupational fashions of the seventies. The doctor costume might be viewed as progress, but Mattel admitted it was added to the line in response to feminist criticism and at the request of their own public relations department (Leavy).

Barbie fashions from the late sixties through the seventies were a non-statement. In contrast, the fashions of the golden age symbolized a nation that valued females as ornaments, consumers, caregivers, and within a limited range, business and professional women.

The Mod outfits, on the other hand, echoed the outer form of the Carnaby Street originals, but to have been a true reflection of society the accessory packs should have contained miniature birth control pill dispensers and marijuana cigarettes. Barbie's love beads and fringed hippie vests were a sanitized imitation of those worn by the real flower children. The doll copied the outer forms while upholding the status quo.

Barbie's world betrayed no sign of a nation struggling with the changing role of women, the drug culture, and the Vietnam War. Hers was always a world of fun whether in the Country Camper or the funky Country Living Home, both manifestations of the good life, California style. Mattel shunned making social statements. Imagine a magazine editor costume inspired by Gloria Steinem; unthinkable. To its credit, however, Mattel did bring black dolls into the line in 1968, during the civil rights movement, a smart marketing ploy as well as the socially responsible thing to do.

Despite the tremendous social changes within the doll's "lifetime," and despite a strong feminist movement, the female-as-ornament attitude prevailed in the Superstar Barbie of 1977. As the name implied, Barbie was now a celebrity in her own right. The new face was somewhat more mature. Most of the fashions were sexy and inappropriate for activities other than lounging or black tie affairs. Fashion Photo, Beauty Secrets, Western, Kissing, and Fashion Jeans Barbies reflected a society preoccupied with self (Fig. 5).

The Fashion Photo and Beauty Secrets dolls, of 1978 and 1980 respectively, were traditional Barbie dolls in that they emphasized glamour. The significance was that an increasing number of versions were offered each year. In 1960, for example, Barbie came in blonde or brunette. Twenty years later, in addition to the Beauty Secrets doll, there was Black Barbie, Hispanic Barbie, Roller Skating Barbie, and three international Barbies in ethnic costumes. Collectively, they cost about $75.

Kissing Barbie debuted in 1979, the doll's twentieth anniversary. By pressing a panel in the back, the doll tilted her head up, pursed her lips, and made a kissing sound. Her dress was a soft pink floral and kissing lips print. After 1977 many of the Barbie versions had a Ken counterpart, but alas there was no Kissing Ken.

Western Barbie appeared in 1981 in the wake of the movie *Urban Cowboy* and rising popular interest in country and western music. Most adults thought the heavy blue eyelids looked sleazy, but girls were fascinated—they could make the doll wink by pressing a panel in the back. Capitalizing on the appeal of horses to young girls, Mattel produced Barbie-scale horses, a horse trailer, and four-wheel drive vehicle to pull it, and Western versions of Ken and Skipper. Horse Lovin' Barbie was produced in 1983 to continue the horse theme.

Fashion Jeans Barbie rode the coattails of the designer jeans craze led by Gloria Vanderbilt and other American designers. More and more, consumers put their faith in designer labels and logos, even on their dolls. Mattel openly exploited this phenomenon by launching the Oscar

Fig. 5 (from left) Fashion Jeans Barbie, Western Barbie, Black Beauty Secrets Barbie, Kissing Barbie, Fashion Photo Barbie.

de la Renta collector series in 1985. The red and gold gown was typical (Fig. 1). A two page color advertisement ran in *Vogue* to let savvy women know that *haute couture* for Barbie was back.

The early eighties' Barbie, in multiple versions and surrounded by accouterments, reflected an ideal that living the good life was its own reward. She was style over substance.

The dressed for success Day-to-Night Barbie of 1985 seemed to be an abrupt change in direction (Fig. 6). She wore the first business attire since "Career Girl." This Barbie was in step with the times. About half of American women were now in the work force, up about 14 percent since 1960 (U.S. Dept. of Commerce).

Perhaps, Mattel recognized this societal change. Tom Wszalek, the company's marketing director for Barbie, indicated that Mattel viewed the Day-to-Night doll as a role model for girls, some of them as young as three when they first played with Barbie. "This doll has a unique play path," he said. "We've made her a woman of substance." (Saari).

It was unlikely, however, that many working women dressed like Barbie. She broke nearly every rule espoused by John Molloy in *The Woman's Dress for Success Book*. Molloy claimed that a conservative suit teamed with plain pumps, natural colored hosiery, and a tailored blouse would establish an air of credibility and authority. Day-to-Night Barbie had the skirted suit, but it was pink, a color forbidden by Molloy

Fig. 6 Day-to-Night Barbies.

(Molloy 53). Pink and white spectator pumps with a matching shoulder bag and brief case completed Barbie's suit.

Day-to-Night Barbie was just the latest in a long pink line of upwardly mobile Barbie dolls. She was the logical descendant of "Career Girl." Both were vague enough to have high play value; any number of business roles from store clerk to head of a corporation was imaginable. The Day-to-Night doll went a step further than her precursor, though. By removing the jacket, reversing the skirt, and changing the shoes, Barbie was ready for a night on the town with Day-to-Night Ken. "Fashion Designer," "Teacher," "TV News Reporter," "Dancer," and "Business

Executive" Day-to-Night outfits could be purchased separately as could the Barbie Home and Office playset.

Day-to-Night Barbie had it all—a career, a man, bliss—and through the costume seemed to tell American girls that they could too. The new slogan was most fitting: "We Girls Can Do Anything—Right, Barbie!"

Since 1959 millions of girls have played with Barbie. Most fondly remember the experience and many saved the dolls as keepsakes of a happy time. But does Barbie hold some deeper meaning? Did she turn a generation of women, now in the prime of life, into plastic bimbos as some critics predicted?

Of course not. Time and again lenders to the 1984 Barbie doll exhibition said that pretending and changing the costumes were the most enjoyable aspects of playing with the doll. Barbie had little influence on their adult lives, but what influence did exist was in the realm of dress. Some felt playing with the doll made them more fashion conscious than they might have been otherwise. An anonymous lender observed: "Our Barbies [referring to her own and her friends'] may have influenced our later lives in that we are now all very fashion conscious, but not trendy. We enjoy make-up, jewelry, nice clothes and good hairstyles." (Anonymous 2). Another lender wrote that Barbie's costumes were the "most exciting concept" of the doll and that years later, "I'm still interested in fashion and I feel that my experiences in selecting Barbie's wardrobe helped nuture (sic) that interest." (Anonymous 3). Kristina Payne offered this insight: "Barbie was a good role model although I don't feel she influenced my life. We imitated with her the life we knew and were creative. If anything, I suppose, she could have brought about a fashion consciousness in my teens."

Playing with Barbie may have had slightly more impact on questionnaire respondents. Even so, a sizeable 48% indicated they felt the doll had no influence on their adult lives. Twenty-seven percent felt Barbie had some influence and the remainder had no feeling either way. In reply to a multiple choice question about what they learned from playing with Barbie, 51% said fashion sense, 21% that society views women as sex objects, and 12% that society views women as consumers. For most, Barbie play was simply a fun experience.

In conclusion, inherent play value is the secret to Barbie's longevity and success. The fashions and accouterments suggest play situations, but children seldom follow adult formulas for having fun. The doll's greatest virtue is her blandness. As one respondent said, "I didn't buy her with a 'built-in' personality." The "We Girls Can Do Anything" slogan is on target.

The doll's ability to impart sexist and materialistic attitudes has been overestimated. True, the doll does convey certain messages, but parents, peers, and institutions such as the school and church, are more effective teachers.

The Barbie doll is, however, an icon of American culture. She represents a society that values females, especially teens and young women, as ornaments, yet simultaneously offers tentative encouragement to explore non-traditional roles. She embodies ambivalent signals that girls should learn to be alluring, but not vulgar; intelligent, but not so much as to threaten men; and to be polite and thoughtful without sharing the limelight. Further, in a society that prizes an affluent lifestyle, Barbie tends to reinforce a belief that wearing the right clothes and acquiring beautiful things will confer status, self-worth, and happiness.

The doll is many things to many people. While feminists generally loathe her, girls adore her. Barbie's negative aspects cannot be denied, but she can be a vehicle for growth. One 32 year old woman, a lender to the museum exhibition summed up the Barbie experience:

Barbie time was my time to be the deciding force in my life. With Barbie I did the things I was not old enough to do in real life. I will always remember the special hours of play with Barbie. She truly let my imagination take flight. (Anonymous 4).

Acknowledgments

Photographs by Marilyn Glander.

Dolls and costumes courtesy of Ashley Lockwood, Barbara Potter, and the Indiana State Museum.

Works Cited

Alexander, Suzanne E. Letter to the author. 12 July 1984.

Anonymous 1. Letter to the author. 14 July 1984.

Anonymous 2. Letter to the author. n.d.

Anonymous 3. Letter to the author. n.d.

Anonymous 4. Letter to the author. n.d.

Barbie Through the Years. Hawthorne, Ca.: Mattel Toys, Inc., 1984.

Billy Boy. *Barbie: Her Life and Times.* New York: Crown Publishers, Inc., 1987.

DeWein, Sibyl and Joan Ashabraner. *The Collectors Encyclopedia of Barbie Dolls and Collectibles.* Paducah, Kentucky: Collector Books, 1971.

Howell, Chauncey. "Barbie Go Home," *Women's Wear Daily.* 19 Dec. 1966: 4-5.

Irving, Candace (Mattel public relations dept.). Letter to Elaine Patton (Indiana State Museum public relations dept.) 5 July 1984.

Kehlbeck, Liz. Letter to the author, n.d.

Leavy, Jan. "Is There a Barbie Doll in Your Past," *Ms.* Sept. 1979: 102.

Molloy, John T. *The Woman's Dress for Success Book.* Chicago: Follett Publishing Co., 1977.

"The Barbie-Doll Set," *The Nation* 27 Apr. 1964: 407.

Payne, Kristina. Letter to the author. 25 June 1984.

Saari, Laura. "A Woman of the '80s, but Still a California Girl," *Orange County Register.* 3 Mar. 1985: H3.

U.S. Dept. of Commerce, Bureau of the Census. *We, the American Women.* Washington: U.S. Government Printing Office, 1984: 7.

Vogue Oct. 1985: 270-71.

American Denim: Blue Jeans and Their Multiple Layers of Meaning

Beverly Gordon

Blue jeans, the now-ubiquitous denim garments that almost constitute a uniform on high school and college campuses, have been an integral part of the American scene for about 130 years. In that time they have embodied many different messages, and functioned in different ways—as symbols of rebellion; outlets for personal creativity; emblems of up-to-date, fashionable awareness; and as evidence of generational longing and insecurity. Changes in jeans styling, embellishment, and marketing are closely tied to changes in the society as a whole, and these changes serve as a subtle but accurate barometer of trends in contemporary popular culture. The jeans phenomenon merits serious attention on the part of the popular culture scholar.

The Blue Jean as Laborer: The Wild West and the Farmer

Jeans first appeared in their now-familiar form in California in the second half of the 19th century. Levi Strauss, a Bavarian immigrant, came to San Francisco in 1850 with a supply of strong canvas cloth that he hoped to sell to people making tents and wagon covers, but when he saw the kind of hard wear the gold prospectors gave their clothes, he had it made into sturdy pants. "Levi's" were really born when Strauss switched to a heavy denim fabric a few years later. Copper rivets were added at the stress points in 1873 (Ratner 1-2; Shea 31; Brooks 64-5). Jeans first evolved, then, as practical rather than fashionable clothing, and were associated with hard-working physical laborers, especially those from the rough and rugged West. By the early twentieth century, when Levis competed with other brands such as Wrangler and Lee, jeans and related denimwear such as protective overalls were the modal garments for farmers. By 1902 the Sears and Roebuck catalogue offered five different denimwear styles (Rupp 83). Again, individuals who wore these garments were not "fashionable," they were not making a statement of any kind; they were simply choosing serviceable, affordable clothing.

The Blue Jean as Anti-Fashion: The First Association

Jeans were first adopted as a kind of anti-fashion—a conscious,

31

pointed statement that goes against the fashion norm and says, "I am different, I am not like you"—by a group of artists in the Santa Fe area in the 1920s (Brooks 58). Generally well-educated individuals of both sexes took to wearing jeans as a badge of their own group identity and special status. They were identifying themselves with the ruggedness, the directness, and the earthiness of the laborer, and were placing themselves as a part of the Western scene. They also adopted a uni-sex look long before it was the norm.

This group of artists continued to sport jeans in the 1930s, but something of the same impulse was also promulgated in the mainstream fashion world. Levi Strauss executives began encouraging Easterners who were taking the newly-popular "dude ranch" vacations to outfit themselves with jeans or overalls, and the garments even became available for the first time in upscale New York stores. Levi Strauss ran an ad in the April, 1935 *Vogue* that stated, "true Western chic was invented by cowboys" (Brooks 70; Berendt 24). Although the trend did not really take off at this time outside the dude ranch context, this was perhaps the first instance where fashionable consumers were encouraged to take on the aura of a particular lifestyle by wearing jeans.

The Blue Jean as War Hero: Widening the Base of Support

World War II was a turning point for blue jeans in America. Materials were scarce as resources were diverted to the war effort, but with the increasing number of workers in the factories and munitions plants, great quantities of durable work clothes were needed. Jeans were declared "essential commodities," and to serve the needs of thousands of Rosie the Riveters, the Blue Bell company came out with a special Wrangler dungaree style dubbed "the Jeanie" (Brooks 71; Quinn 19; Shea 31). Once again, these were not really fashionable garments—they were work clothes. They were still used only in a particular context. Because factory war work was seen in a positive light, however, the garments were perceived as part of the patriotic, all-pitching-in spirit, and were thought of fondly. To women workers who had been used to wearing dresses and more constricting garments, they must have also seemed liberating and refreshingly comfortable. Wartime fashion was changing, also, and taking much of its detailing from the rather unfashionable wartime scene. Head wraps or turbans, originally used in the factories to keep long hair out of the machinery, became part of acceptable evening wear. Shoulder pads, originally seen in military uniforms, became an indispensable part of women's civilian garments. Jeans were associated with a particular war-era lifestyle, and were poised somewhere in the middle on the fashion/anti-fashion continuum.

The Blue Jean Anti-Fashion: Tomboys, Bad Boys and Bohemians

After the war, jeans were no longer just unfashionable; they came to have widespread distinct anti-fashion associations. The hard-edged, square-shouldered female styles gave way in the high-style world to the ultra-feminine and very dressy "New Look," and the more rugged, unisex denim garments began to be associated with youth, freedom, and rebellion. One of the first things Western American servicemen stationed in Europe did when peace was declared was trade their uniforms for blue jeans. They were free, and they were finished with carrying the burdens of the world. Bennington College students, who were generally known as "artistic" and rather unconventional, adopted jeans as a "virtual uniform" on their Vermont campus (Brooks 58). They too used their clothing to symbolize freedom—freedom from the norms of conventional society.

Sometimes this freedom was simply the prerogative of youth, and was seen as innocent and harmless. Eddie Fisher crooned *Dungaree Doll* in the late 1940s (Rosenberg and Bordow xi), and evoked the image of a happy-go-lucky bobby soxer, a tomboy who would eventually, in the words of another post-war era song, "trade her bobby sox for stockings." Another type of freedom emerged in the early 1950s, however, which was seen as much more sinister. There was a group of disenfranchised individuals who could not find a place in the conformist climate of Cold War America and who reacted to it with alienation and disdain. These were the young people symbolized in Marlon Brando's *The Wild One* and James Dean's *Rebel Without a Cause*, the angry or confused or simply no-good "juvenile delinquents" who at their most extreme flashed switchblades and tire irons and terrorized neighborhoods. These young people, also, wore jeans: jeans and leather jackets were the anti-fashion wardrobe that symbolically flaunted the mores of the frightened society at large. Jeans were so strongly associated with these outcasts, in fact, that a 1959 movie about an unwed teenage mother was tellingly titled *Blue Denim* (Shea 30). The good-versus-bad connations were symbolized by a "dress right" campaign launched by the American Institute of Men's and Boy's Wear and aimed particularly at blue jeans (Brooks 72).

Associations with the wild west actually strengthened or reinforced the anti-fashion statement that jeans made in the 1950s. This was the era of the Gray Flannel Suit and the Organization Man;[1] it was a time permeated by what author Peter Beagle characterizes as "a strangled, constipated idea of a proper life" (Beagle 14). It was also the era of the Hollywood and TV Western. Good and bad cowboys were sometimes differentiated by the color of their hats, but they all wore jeans. The Western simultaneously replayed the good guys/bad guys scenario of the Cold War and represented an escape from it, a foray into a still wild or "untamed" past where people did not have to fit into such carefully prescribed niches. Baby-boom children who grew up with Western heroes grew up with images of jeans, and wore them for their creative play. They wore them when they wanted to step into a fantasy world that was outside the world of piano lessons, visiting relatives and other dutiful activities.

Anti-Fashion at its Peak: The "Jeaning of America" and the Personalized Jean

It was in the 1960s that the "jeaning of America" occurred, and jeans took on a new role. The first signs of the shift really began in the late 1950s, when another type of rebel, the bohemian or "beatnik," began to adopt them with black sweaters for everyday wear. Unlike the Brando/Dean "bad boy" rebel, this was a dissenter, an urban intellectual who came to an anti-fashion statement of this sort from a thought-out position about the materialistic, conformist society of the day. To wear plain jeans and dark colors was to reject the more-is-better, new-is-better mentality of the Organization Man world. 1962, according to Levi Strauss executive Alfred Sanguinetti, marked the "breakout" point in jeans sales, with sales figures doubling in just three years. They further quintupled between 1965 and 1970 (Brooks 73-74).[2] By 1967 the anti-fashion statement was screaming across the land, for jeans were one of the most visible symbols of the rapidly increasing numbers of disenfranchised youth. The late 1960s were, of course, the turbulent period in which there was a marked escalation of the undeclared war in Vietnam, a war that polarized the society and led to a widespread rejection of mainstream social norms on the part of the younger generation. The youth-dominated counterculture, which was made up of the same baby-boomers who had worn jeans as play clothes and had grown up with James Dean and other such cultural icons, turned to jeans very naturally. Jeans were practical, long-lasting, and unchanging; they were the very antitheses of the mainstream "straight" world where fashion was by its very nature ever-changing and quickly obsolescent. They were cheap, comfortable, and associated with physicality; they represented freedom from dutifulness, and because they were simultaneously associated with work and play, came to stand for a society where there really was no distinction between the two. As Valerie Carnes put it in a 1977 article entitled "Icons of Popular Fashion,"

Denim jeans became [in the 1960s] the ultimate no-fashion put-down style—a classless, cheap, unisex look that stood for, variously, frontier values, democracy, plain living, ecology and health, rebellion *a la* Brando or Dean, a new interest in the erotic import of the pelvis, or, as Charles Reich suggests in *The Greening of America*, a deliberate rejection of the "artificial plastic-coated look" of the affluent consumer society. (237)

Jeans may have been the common anti-fashion denominator among the young, but all jeans were not alike. Jeans wearers avoided the plastic veneer and the sameness and artificiality it represented by the very act of wearing their jeans. Jeans conformed more and more to their own particular body shapes as they were worn and washed (cotton denim shrinks and stretches each time it is washed and reworn). Over time jeans came to carry particular "scars"—stains, rips, frayed areas, patches—that could be associated with remembered events and experiences. A pair of jeans became intensely personal. If a small hole developed it might be left alone as a "badge" of experience, or great deliberation might go into the choice of an appropriate fabric with which to cover it. Soon, counterculture youth were *glorifying* their jeans—decorating and embellishing them, making them colorful and celebratory, and making them into visible, vocal personal statements. Silk, velvet, leather, feathers, bells, beads, rivets, sequins, paint—anything that could be applied to denim fabric was applied to someone's jeans, jeans jackets, and related accessories. Men who had never learned to sew and who under most circumstances would think of embroidery as unmanly learned the necessary stitches to work on their own clothes. The unisex garment that symbolized the alternative youth culture was an appropriate vehicle for the breakdown of gender roles, and besides, one's jeans were too personal to trust to anyone else. By 1974 imaginatively adorned jeans were such a pervasive and interesting phenomenon that the Levi Strauss company sponsored a national "denim art" contest and was deluged with entries. Entrants repeatedly stated that they found it difficult to part with the garments long enough for them to be displayed in the exhibition; they felt they were giving up a part of themselves. "I feel most myself when I have my jeans on" was a typical comment from an entrant. "My jeans are an extension of me"; "my shorts [are] my autobiography on denim" (Beagle 14,73).

The Blue Jean as Fashion: Absorbing the Counter-Culture With a Designer Label

In some ways it had by this time become almost necessary to dramatically personalize one's jeans in order to still make an anti-fashion statement. Many of the outward signs and even some of the underlying ideas of the counterculture had been adopted (some might say usurped) by the mainstream culture at large. Blue jeans in and of themselves were so well accepted in the establishment that even such political figures as New York City mayor John Lindsay and presidential candidate Jimmy Carter were happy to be photographed wearing them. Anti-fashion had not only been absorbed by fashion, but had become part of its very essence. John Brooks, writing in *The New Yorker* in 1979, attributed the fashionable usurpation of the jeans phenomenon to the early 1970s "search for the fountain of youth" (Brooks 60), but it may have been as much a sign of an underlying widespread hunger for life-affirming values in what was a confused and dark time.

Jeans and other denim garments were also seen in the early 1970s as quintessentially *American*. Jeans had been developed in the United States, of course, and had long carried associations of the American West, but once they had filtered into the international fashion scene, they came to stand for the country as a whole. In 1973 the American Fashion Critics presented a special award to Levi Strauss for "a fundamental American fashion that...now influences the world." Nieman Marcus also gave Levi Strauss its Distinguished Service in Fashion Award that same year (Carnes 236).[3] The popular press began to print rhetorical questions like, "after all, what's more American than denim?" ("Do It Up Denim!" 142) and in 1974 American Motors Corporation contracted with Levi Strauss to provide blue denim fabric for upholstery for its Gremlin and Hornet cars (Fehr 73). The Gremlin, which was promoted as America's answer to the Volkswagon beetle, was meant to be both upbeat and patriotic, and denim furnishings were thought to communicate both qualities.

Jeans sales continued to climb. By 1977 over 500 million pairs were sold in this country alone—more than twice the number of the total population (Brooks 58).

Fashion and anti-fashion came exceedingly close during this period, but there were continually two thrusts to the jeans craze. The counter-culture continued to thrive and maintained and fostered a do-your-own, personalize-your-clothing vision. Numerous instruction books were published between 1973 and 1977 that carried a power-to-the-people message and told people how to fashion and re-fashion their own denim clothing. Publications with such titles as *Clothing Liberation*, and *Make it in Denim, The Jeans Scene, The Jeans Book,* and *Native Funk and Flash* (Harlow; Jacopetti; Johnson; Rosenberg and Weiner; Todhunter; Torbet) continued to advocate inexpensive and comfortable clothing that made use of worn garments and other available materials. Cast-offs and odds and ends could not only be salvaged, but creatively used.

At the same time, there was a high-fashion version of this democratic, anti-fashion trend. Couturiers who saw these creative outfits on the streets and in such legitimizing exhibitions as Wesleyan University's "Smart Ass Art" (1973) and Levi Strauss' "Denim Art" at the Museum of Contemporary Crafts (1974) moved in and produced their own high-style versions of counter-culture styles. Givenchy designed an entire denim wardrobe for film star Audrey Hepburn, for example, and Giorgio outfitted Dyan Cannon and Ava Gardner (Fehr 55, 66; Shea 29). A $2,325 denim-lined mink jacket and mink-cuffed jeans were shown on the fashion runways in Paris in 1974, and professionally-designed embroidered, sequinned and nail-studded ensembles were going for about $500 in New York boutiques (Fehr 27, 45). Recycled and well-worn fabrics—hallmarks of the counter-culture look—were part of this style. Giorgio's jeans outfits that sold for $250 were made from already-used denim, for example, and designer shops in department stores like Lord and Taylor sold recycled jeans for three times the price of new ones (Fehr 46).

By the late 1970s, when the baby-boomer generation had been largely absorbed into the work force and the responsibilities of parenting, and the counter-culture vision had become diffused, the high-style fashion forces won out over the anti-fashion style. Couture denim filtered down into the ready-to-wear market. Designer labels became an obsession; "designer jeans" were " *the* pants in America," according to a Saks Fifth Avenue retailer. Calvin Klein, who drew attention to jeans sporting his label with an erotic advertising campaign, sold 125,000 pairs a week in 1979 (McCord 115). Designer jeans were in such demand that there was a thriving counterfeit trade, and by 1981 *Good Housekeeping* magazine ran a feature advising consumers how to make sure they were buying the "real thing" (202)[4]

Designer jeans were often based on anti-fashion prototypes (both Calvin Klein and Oscar de la Renta are known to have sent photographers out into the streets of New York to document what people were wearing) (Carnes 235-36), but they tended to be subtle: they did not, in the early Reagan era, generally sport embroidered patches and tattered fringe. Often nearly indistinguishable (except by the small designer label sewn on the back pocket), they offered ostentatious but restrained snob appeal. Jeans were no longer the "great American equalizer;"[5] homemade and recycled garments did not have a place in this less democratic age— or rather, they had a place, but it was back with the poor and have-nots. Designer jeans were made to fit and flatter the body, but they were made to be long lasting and uniform rather than to age and change with the individual. In 1984 several fabric manufacturers came out with new polyester/denim blends that were intended to stretch with the body and keep their shape. The Sydeco company introduced "Forever Blue," a new fade-resistant jeans fabric that was designed to "look new longer" ("Institute Report" 124).

The Blue Jean as Fashion: Pre-Packaged Experience

The Aged Jean. It seems fitting to begin the most recent chapter of the jeans saga in 1985, with the story of "The Authentic Stone." This was a product developed by Mr. Marshall Banks, who got the idea when he discovered a small piece of pumice stone in the pocket of his newly-purchased jeans. Banks learned that the stone was accidentally left behind from the "stone washing"—the preconditioning process—that the jeans had been subjected to. Small pieces of pumice, which is an abrasive material, had been added to a pre-market wash in order to soften the garment.[6] As the earlier description of innovative 1984 jeans fabrics makes clear, stone-washing and other preconditioning treatments were not yet *de rigueur*. Banks stated, presumably with his tongue in his cheek, that he hoped to appeal to the "do-it-yourselfer" with his Authentic [pumice] Stone packaged in its own "bed of denim." He felt his product blended "the whole 60s look with a status connotation"; it was a symbolic pre-packaging of experience, a fashionable way of referring to the anti-fashion of the past. One hundred thousand Authentic Stones had been sold to leading department stores by 1986 ("A Six Dollar Stone Wash" 77).

The 1960s anti-fashion style had indeed been a look of well-used, lived-in jeans. The Vietnam years were enormously intense—every day brought the promise of incredible revelation or impending apocalypse[7]—and experience was highly charged. The jeans one wore were part of the experience; they were faithful companions, they had been there. Even if they weren't heavily decorated, they were "encrusted" with memories (Fehr 11), and held the accumulated charge.[8] Small wonder that aged, faded, tattered jeans were treasured: they were not only comfortable, but were far richer and more meaningful than those that were new and unmarked.

The best jeans were those that had aged naturally, over the course of time and experience, but there were numerous home-grown or do-it-yourself methods to speed up the aging process in order to look presentable. Folk wisdom suggested the best way to soften and shape one's jeans was to repeatedly get them wet and wear them until they dried. This could be done by soaking in the bathtub, but the sun-and-salt-water of the ocean beach environment was much preferred.[9] New jeans were also home-treated by rubbing sandpaper and pumice stones across the fabric, by burying them, or by adding washing soda or bleach to a tubful of water (Beagle 39-40; Fehr 62-4). The bleach treatment was more controversial, largely because it weakened the fabric in the wrong places, and looked bleached rather than worn (Todhunter 26-7).

The faded look was commercially imitated in a pre-bleached fabric for the first time in 1969, presumably inspired by the sun-bleached denims seen on the Riviera, and the look was popular in France (Carnes 235; McCord 115). Some very high-priced customized jeans were pre-faded; items taken to "Robbie's Stud and Rhinestone Shop," an establishment that serviced fashion-conscious celebrities in Los Angeles, for example, were sent to a denim fading lab before the studding process began (Fehr 55). A few American laundry companies developed fading treatments in 1973 and jeans manufacturers like H. D. Lee contracted with them for several thousand faded garments (Fehr 64; Koshetz 47), but bleached fabrics were still not the norm. More and more "pre-washed" denims were on the market by the late 1970s, but the phenomenon crept in slowly. A 1981 *Mademoiselle* fashion column spoke of the "new, faded look," but disparaged it for its extra costliness. Readers were advised to use inexpensive commercial color removers or fading products on their jeans if they liked the look of prewashed fabric ("Denims: Here's How..." 258).

The prewashed look was characteristic of jeans manufactured by Guess, Inc., a company started in 1981, interestingly enough, by four brothers who had emigrated to the United States from France. Guess jeans achieved their well-worn look through a stonewashing process that took up to 12 hours, and by 1986 the company was already having trouble finding launderers with whom they could subcontract, as the treatments were breaking even the strongest washing machines (Ginsberg 4-5). Guess products, though expensive, began "flying off department store shelves" almost as soon as they were stocked (Slutsker 210), and Guess captured a significant piece of the youth market by the mid 1980s. Other companies quickly found ways to emulate the prewashed look. *Rolling Stone* magazine proclaimed in May of 1986 that the "best jeans available" were triple bleached and double stonewashed (Schecter 67-71), but the sentiment was still by no means universally accepted. One commentator writing in *Esquire* protested that hastening the aging process was a form of "faddish dishonesty." "To wear jeans is to create a life mold of oneself in denim," he exclaimed; pre-worn jeans are not a reflection of the "person within" (Berendt 25). Numerous "upscale" American designers were using denim in their new lines, but were concentrating on less casual items such as dresses and coats, and aging treatments were not part of their design process (Goodman 48-51; "Designing the Blues," 78-9; La Ferla 60; "Denim Rides Again" 76-8).

The Guess prototype and its "worn to death" look[10] continued to permeate the retail denim market, however, and it has effectively dominated the 1987-1988 fashion season. With fierce competition for the many dollars spent on jeans and other denim items (more than thirteen pairs of jeans were sold every second in 1986) ("Denim Rides Again" 76) it is not surprising that novelty would be at a premium, but there is another, more fundamental reason that such products caught on. The contemporary crop of worn and faded looking denimwear provides its primarily young customers with a costume that has *lived*. It carries a feeling or ambiance, an illusion of experience. It, even more seriously than the Authentic Stone, represents a pre-packaged kind of experience that is risk-free.[11]

The actual intense and heady experiences of the counter-culture Vietnam generation are not available to today's youth. "Free love" and easy sexuality have been tainted by the terrifying fear of AIDS, and optimistic faith in expanded consciousness through mind-altering drugs has been destroyed by the spectre of crack and other lethal substances.

The world no longer seems full of unending promise. It is no longer possible to take to the road with the certainty that there will be "brothers" who will provide places to stay along the way; this is the age of the homeless, and people avert their eyes. The realities of child abuse, incest, alcoholism and family violence are ever-more evident. There is no groundswell of passionate feeling to tap into, no clear vision of a better future. Unlike the children of the 1960s, then, the children of the 1980s are cautious, and rightfully afraid. I maintain that they have taken to the washed-out tattered garments because they *imply* experience, adventure and drama, and offer a vicarious (though not really conscious) experience of it. These clothes provide the security of the most up-to-date fashion, but the fashion itself alludes to anti-fashion of an earlier time, and plays upon a longing for the (counter) culture that produced it.

Distressed Denim. The terms used to describe the new denimwear are quite telling. Denim is now subjected not only to stones, but to acid; it is "abused," "distressed," "sabotaged" and "blasted"; it has been "washed out." It is also cold and frigid: it is "frosted," "frozen out," and "iced"; and "glacier" or "polar-washed." At first these terms seemed reminiscent of the words used in the Vietnam era for the drug experience ("stoned," "wasted," "wiped out"), but in reality they have a much harder, more anguished edge. One was stoned or wiped out from an abundance of experience; now one has simply weathered the storm ("Storm Riders," and "White Lightening" are two contemporary jeans styles). Today's "Get Used" fashions echo the underlying desperation of the age.

Descriptive labels that come with this aged denimwear try to be comforting. "This garment is made to look used and soft," one states. "It is broken in just for you." Customers are reassured that the jeans are "inspired by the faded, comfortable character of well worn clothing," or by the "comfortable good looks and free-wheeling spirit of aviators and prairie hands." This is "authentic apparel," state the labels; these garments are "like three years old." The underlying message is that the world out there is a tough one, but the clothing has been through it and has already taken it. It is protective, for it acts as a foil and absorbs the shock so its owner doesn't have to. It is soothing: "worn denim is man's best friend."[12]

The 1988 season denimwear also borrows from the free-spirited, make-your-own, recycle-it trend of the mid 1970s. Couturiers were beginning to show this look about two years ago, but now increasing numbers of ready-to-wear garments are designed so as to look as if they were made from several pairs of cut-up and reused jeans. There are waistband details tucked into bodices or turned upside-down on the bottom of jackets; there are odd pockets and belt loops sewn in at jaunty diagonal angles. Contrasting color patches, particularly in mattress ticking prints, are also evident.

Sadly, all of these trendy looks are mere facades. Pre-washed jeans are not really made "just for" anyone; they hold no one's individual contours. Jackets may have extra waistbands and added pockets or patches, but they do not have the free-spirited spontaneity and freshness of the make-your own era. Much of the tattered quality of contemporary denimwear, also, looks contrived and unnatural. Wear and tear that develops during consecutive hours of laundering does not necessarily occur in areas that would be naturally stressed or worn, and sewn-in fringed selvages look too regular to be real. When a whole line of jackets even bears a "rip" in the same place and the rip is always outlined with rows of stitches, the point is exceedingly forced. These clothes may at first allude to another era, and may offer the illusion of experience and comfort, but illusions are all they offer. They are in reality pre-packaged, just like the Authentic Stone. They set up a facade for their wearers, a facade that makes them seem larger than they may be able to be. The look has struck a responsive chord, for it speaks to a yearning on the part of the young jeans customer, a yearning for a time when the world was not just tough, but exciting, and full of promise and imminent discovery.

Selling the Image. Photographs used in magazine advertisements for this denim clothing support the thesis developed above. Jeans manufacturers take it for granted at this point that their product is desirable, but struggle to create memorable images that prospective customers will identify with. Consequently, the photographs do not feature the garments as much as create a mood or tell a story. The stories are dreamy and "mythic" (Conant 64)[13] and full of implication. Sometimes they imply a free and uninhibited sexuality—Calvin Klein ads featuring photographs by Bruce Weber consist of ambiguous images such as one woman surrounded by four men, two of whom are shirtless, or an odd tangle of bodies on the grass. Guess advertisements often include unbuttoned and unbuckled garments, and glimpses of lacy underwear beneath. A recent Jordache ad was headlined, "I Can't Get No Satisfaction," and simulated a young man's internal monologue: "I don't know what's with you girls...Your body says yes but your lips say no...but you, Sandy, you're not like the rest. You wouldn't play with my head..." The story had a happy ending, for in the next frame Sandy and the young man are entwined together, and he is peering soulfully into her denim jacket. Even where there is no explicit sexuality, there is a sensual undertone. Characters in Guess ads are always positioned suggestively, leaning, stretching or slouching with studied ease.

Many of the vignettes include references to the adventurous past of the blue jean. There are couples leaning on motorcycles (Calvin Klein) and men in black leather gloves (Guess); rugged rodeo riders or freewheeling Western characters with bolo ties or bandana neckerchiefs (Guess, Levis); and even a young girl with a head kerchief that looks as if she just stepped off the wagon train (Guess). There are aviators and wavy-haired workers from the World War II era (Work Force—the Gap), and sullen bohemian-types dressed in black (Calvin Klein).

The characters in these advertisements are uniformly young and attractive, but they rarely seem full of vitality, joy or optimism. Often, they face completely away from the camera or have their faces totally or partially obscured by unkept long hair (itself a reference to the 1960s) or by shadow. Where faces are visible, expressions tend to be enigmatic: dreamy or thoughtful, perhaps, or petulant, sad, or weary. This enigmatic quality is quite anonymous, and suitably enough it allows potential customers to project themselves into the scene and become one of the characters. The scenes hint, in a rather desultory way, of experience and adventure, and imply that the worn garments the characters wear will bring that experience within the reach of even the most unadventurous or inexperienced teenager.

Blue jeans and related denim garments have, in sum, come to stand not just for the Wild West or the rugged laborer or the hardworking farmer—they have become an integral part of the whole American (and perhaps the world-wide) scene. They have been bleached, ripped, washed with acid, washed with stones, patched, cut up, decorated, distressed, and "worn to death," but they are resilient, and seem to always be able to return in yet another guise and take on yet another layer of meaning. They have at different times seemed matter-of-fact and part of the scenery, and at other times have called out for notice and attention. They have served both as symbols of the culture at large and of subsets of that culture, and of rebellious, outspoken counterculture groups; they have been fashionable, unfashionable, and hallmarks of anti-fashion. They have embodied many of the longings, beliefs and realities of the generations that have worn them. We must watch and try to understand them as they continue to evolve.

Notes

[1] See Russell (48) for a discussion of the gray flannel suit imagery. The movie by that name came out in 1957. See also William Hollingsworth Whyte, *The Organization Man.* (New York: Simon & Shuster, 1956)

[2] Brooks reports that the Levi Strauss company commissioned a survey in 1965 that indicated most people still associated the jeans with farmers, but the turning point in the popular association must have occurred very shortly thereafter.

[3]Alison Lurie (87) later came to attribute the popularity of Levis in Europe to the belief among European teens that "the power and virtue of America" was contained in the jeans, and would rub off on anyone who wore them.

[4]Counterfeiting of jeans had actually begun some time before this date, with the bulk of the bogus products going overseas. Thirty-five thousand pairs of forged Levis and Wrangler label jeans were confiscated in West Germany in 1977. See "West Germany: A Booming Market in Counterfeit Jeans" (38-9).

[5]This epithet (and a similar one, the "great common denominator") had been bandied about considerably in the late 1960s and early 1970s. See Fehr 35, Shea 29.

[6]Fehr claims (63) that the original derivation of the phrase "stone wash" comes from a pre-industrial era when garments were softened by a long exposure to running water. The garments were buried in streams, she says, and held down by rocks or stones. I have been unable to confirm this explanation, and rather suspect it is more likely related to the fact that fabric was long cleaned by rubbing over stones in the stream beds.

[7]I speak from memory.

[8]The thesis that clothing and other objects can hold a psychic charge has been developed at length by Mihaly Csikszentmihalyi and Eugene Rochberg-Halton in *The Meaning of Things: Domestic Symbols and the Self*. Although this feeling about jeans was probably at its strongest in the Vietnam era when the jeans were still symbolic of counterculture beliefs, it has clearly not died out. In 1985 sculptor Bob Edlund offered to preserve the spirit of ones jeans forever by "freezing" them in characteristic poses with several coats of fiberglass resin. Edlund said he came up with this idea because jeans "are the hardest things in the world to part with." He even planned to coat children's overalls in this manner, much in the spirit of bronzed baby shoes. See *People* ("For A Mere $1,250" 79).

[9]Brooks claims (80) he was given this advice when he bought his first pair of jeans in 1979; jeans "connoisseurs" had the benefit of years of experience when they told him what to do. Beagle also discusses this process at length (39-40).

[10]This was the actual phrase used by *Rolling Stone* fashion editor Laurie Schecter (68).

[11]It is somewhat outside the parameters of the jeans story, but another type of fashion that caught on in the mid 1980s was the safari-look, made up primarily of cotton khaki garments. The look was spurred on by such popular movies as the "Raiders of the Lost Ark" and "Out of Africa," but it was first marketed by an innovative company named Banana Republic. When it was a new company, Banana Republic bought up lots of used army and safari clothing and restyled them for its customers. (See feature program on specialty retailers, *Adam Smith's Moneyworld*, airing on P.B.S. network T.V., October, 1986). These safari-type clothes also provided a safe fantasy—a vicarious sense of adventure.

[12]These adjectives and statements were all copied from labels on denimwear found in a variety of department stores in Madison, Wisconsin in February, 1988.

[13]There are even some jeans advertisements that are framed and titled, like slice-of-life or art photographs. *Seventeen* magazine carried an ad for Jeanjer denimwear in September, 1986, for example, that featured a snapshot-like image of a sensual girl in jeans and a denim jacket, outlined in black and clearly set off against the page. It was captioned, "'Desert Blues', 1986."

Works Cited

Beagle, Peter. *American Denim: A New Folk Art.* (Presented by Richard M. Owens and Tony Lane) New York: Harry N. Abrams, 1975.

Berendt, John. "Blue Jeans," *Esquire* September 1986: 24-6.

Brooks, John. "Annals of Business: A Friendly Product, *New Yorker* 12 November 1979: 58-80.

Carnes, Valerie. "Icons of Popular Fashion," *Icons of America*, Ray N. Browne and Marshall Fishwick, eds. Bowling Green, Ohio: Bowling Green State University Popular Press, 1978: 228-240.

Conant, Jennet. "Sexy Does It," *Newsweek* 15 September 1986: 64.

Csikszentmihalyi, Mihaly and Eugene Rochberg-Halton. *The Meaning of Things: Domestic Symbols and the Self.* Cambridge: Cambridge University Press, 1981.

"Denim Rides Again," *Life* September 1986: 76-8.

"Denims: Here's How to Buy the Best and Fade Them Fast," *Mademoiselle* August 1981: 258.

"Designing the Blues," *New York* 17 November 1986: 78-9.

"Do it up Denim!" *Mademoiselle* February 1978: 140-44.

Fehr, Barbara. *Yankee Denim Dandies.* Blue Earth, Minn.: Piper Press, 1974.

"For a Mere $1,250, Sculptor Bob Edlund Will See to it that Your Jeans Never Wear Out," *People* 11 November 1985: 79.

Ginsburg, Steve. "Despite a Feud, Marcianos Make Guesswork Pay," *Women's Wear Daily* 25 November 1986: 4-5.

Good Housekeeping April 1981: 202.

Goodman, Wendy. "Upscale Blues," *New York* 10 February 1986: 48-51.

Harlow, Eve. *The Jeans Scene.* New York: Drake, 1973.

"Institute Report: Denim Update," *Good Housekeeping* September 1984: 124.

Jacopetti, Alexandra. *Native Funk and Flash.* San Francisco: Scrimshaw Press, 1974.

Johnson, Jann. *The Jeans Book.* New York: Ballantine Press, 1972.

Koshetz, Herbert. "Laundry Offers New Way to Age Jeans," *New York Times* 7 August, 1973: 47.

La Ferla, Ruth. "Singing the Blues," *New York Times Magazine*, 13 July 1986, Section 6: 60.

Lurie, Alison. *The Language of Clothes.* New York: Random House, 1981.

McCord, Jacqueline. "Blue Jean Country," *New York Times Magazine* 29 April 1979: 115.

Quinn, Carin C. "The Jeaning of America—and the World," *American Heritage* April 1978: 14-21.

Ratner, Elaine, "Levi's," *Dress* 1 (1975): 1-5.

Riesman, David. *The Lonely Crowd: A Study of the Changing American Character.* Garden City: Doubleday, 1953.

Rosenberg, Sharon and Joan Wiener Bordow. *The Denim Book.* Englewood Cliffs, N.J.: Prentice Hall, 1978.

Rosenberg, Sharon and Joan Wiener. *The Illustrated Hassle-Free Make Your Own Clothes Book.* San Francisco: Straight Arrow Press, 1971.

Rupp, Becky. "In Praise of Bluejeans: The Denimization of America," *Blair Ketchum's Country Journal* December 1985: 82-6.

Russell, Douglas A. *Costume History and Style.* Englewood Cliffs, N. J.: Prentice-Hall, 1983.

Schecter, Laurie. "Red-Hot Blues," *Rolling Stone* 8 May 1986: 67-71.

Shea, Robert. "Yesterday's Leggings Are Today's Fashion Craze," *Today's Health* March 1975: 29.

"A Six Dollar Stone Wash," *Newsweek* 22 September 1986: 77.

Slutsker, Gary. "The Smoking Bun," *Forbes* 25 March 1985: 210.

Todhunter, Hazel. *Make it in Denim*. New York: Taplinger, 1977.

Torbet, Laura. *Clothing Liberation: Or Out of the Closet and Into the Streets*. New York: Ballantine Press, 1973.

"West Germany: A Booming Market in Counterfeit Jeans," *Business Week* 8 August 1977: 37-38.

Black Sororities and Fraternities:
A Case Study in Clothing Symbolism

Lillian O. Holloman

In the United States, clothing is commonly used to indicate affiliation with a group, an organization, or an activity. Such association is very evident in Black Greek letter organizations. Like many segments of popular culture, Black sororities and fraternities are examples of a subcultural group that is greatly characterized by its distinctive dress. The linkage between dress and Black Greek letter organizations is rooted in history.

Because Blacks have historically derived their sense of importance from family, friends, and group affiliation, membership in Greek letter organizations offered Blacks not only a sense of belonging but the opportunity to create symbols that reflected their group affiliation. Thus, Black Greek letter organizations made themselves quite visible on college campuses because of their conspicuous, even flamboyant display of apparel and other items of adornment. It is the flamboyant quality that distinguishes the dress of Black sorority and fraternity members from that of their white counterparts. Such conspicuous display is at least in part related to the forces that propelled the formation of Greek letter organizations during the early decades of this century.

Black Greek Letter Organizations

The first Black Greek letter organization started on a white college campus in 1906 at Cornell University. Black students felt the need for an organization that would respond to the isolation and alienation that they were experiencing. This resulted in the formation of a fraternity whose goal was to foster unity, support, and academic excellence among its members. These same goals precipitated the formation of additional Black Greek letter organizations on other white campuses. Visible signs of group membership strengthened the bonds among the members and contributed to the growth and solidarity of their organization.

Black sororities and fraternities began on historically Black college campuses at about the same time that they began on white college campuses. Their formation on Black campuses was, however, not a result

46

of racial isolation in the campus community but the result of isolation of another kind—exclusion from the mainstream of society. Black students needed to feel connected on a broader level. Greek letter organizations provided a channel for Black college students to transcend geographical barriers in uniting with others holding similar values and goals.

The commitment for continued unity toward their goals triggered the formation of "post-college" or graduate chapters of Black sororities and fraternities. Coupled together, the college and graduate chapters worked relentlessly to provide Blacks with a support network throughout the country. Such support was especially beneficial to Blacks as they migrated and sought employment in towns where they had neither family nor friends. They could depend on Black fraternities and sororities to provide services that were generally unavailable to Blacks. Such traditional resources as life insurance and employment information were often the results of networking from within these Greek organizations. Thus, social action on behalf of minorities became a distinguishing characteristic of the Black Greek letter organization. Because of their unique bonding and purpose, Black Greek letter organizations continued to prosper decade after decade.

During the turbulent 60s and early 70s, however, there was a definite wane in their popularity as scores of new Black organizations sprang up to attract the attention of the masses of Blacks who were involved in social action. While still involved in eradicating society's ills, Black Greeks were not viewed as the preeminent channels of collective action as they had been in the past.

Now that the 60s and 70s are behind, and many of the competing organizations are now defunct, there has been a resurgence of Black Greek letter organizations throughout the country. Once again, Black fraternities and sororities serve a special role on the college campus. They are again highly visible because of their conspicuous dress and adornment.

Clothing Symbolism

Symbolic interaction theory proposes that symbols which have shared meaning are used to communicate nonverbally with others (Kaiser 184-85). For Black sororities and fraternities, clothing and its adornment and accessories are the major symbols used in nonverbal communication: they are used to show group affiliation and group exclusion; they serve as quasi-uniforms; they are used to highlight such special activities as the pledge period, rituals, and political events.

Group Affiliation. In the case of the Black Greek letter organization, each group is distinguished by the unique symbols that are incorporated into its wardrobe: its colors, mascot, crest, and letters of the Greek alphabet. Anyone wearing either of these latter three symbols communicates an affiliation with a particular sorority or fraternity. These emblems are usually worn imprinted on hats, T-shirts, sweaters, jackets, or items of ornamentation such as pins, pendants, earrings and bracelets. These symbols so strongly imply sorority or fraternity membership that it is an offense to wear them if one is not a member of the sorority or fraternity that is represented by the emblems. The offending party is subject to being punished by having the emblem physically removed by a Greek representative of that particular group.

"Color" is also a strong Greek indicator. Color is so closely associated with a specific group that non-members wearing the colors might constantly be asked, "Are you a Delta?" or "Are you a Zeta?" Certainly, if one observes two or more students assembled, all wearing the colors associated with a Greek organization, it is assumed that the students are members of the Greek organization. This assumption is made even in the absence of other identifying insignia.

Group Exclusion. Just as dress and adornment communicate group affiliation for the Black fraternity or sorority member, it also exemplifies group exclusion. It sends out a clear message that certain individuals have been chosen—"selected" from the masses to be part of a highly visible and highly desirable group. Wearing the garb of their Greek organization sets them apart from the non-members, excluding those who desired to pledge but were not selected. In fact, many critics of fraternities and sororities cite their exclusivity as one of the negative aspects of "Greekdom," contending that Greek organizations are elitist and serve only as divisive forces among college students.

Therefore, as the foregoing discussion suggests, donning the attire which reflects Greek organizational membership demonstrates exclusivity which may be viewed as positive in terms of the psychological lift of being "chosen" or can be negative in terms of the schism created between those who are and those who are not chosen to be part of that organization.

Black Greek Clothing as a Quasi-Uniform. A quasi-uniform is similar to a formal uniform except that it is slightly less regimented. It allows for some individual variation with a limited range of possible deviations. Like the formal uniform, the quasi-uniform is an emblem of an organization and it tends to suppress individuality (Joseph 66).

The clothing of Black Greeks can be classified as a quasi-uniform. It serves to identify membership in a Greek organization, and is informal in general attire, requiring a lesser degree of conformity than a bona-fide uniform. There is much similarity in the choice of clothing worn among members of the same sorority or fraternity even though there is allowable flexibility and individuality within the broad range of conformity. When a fraternity performs publicly, each member may be technically dressed differently, while wearing enough of the same symbols that similarity in dress is quite obvious. Like a formal uniform, a quasi-uniform suppresses the individuality of a Greek member while focusing on the common characteristics of the group. A clear example can be noticed where group stereotypes are often perpetuated by non-Greek individuals, while the traits and characteristics of a single Greek member are often overlooked. Examples of existing stereotypic traits are: If an individual is a "Q," he likes to party; if he is an Alpha, he is a scholar; if he is a Kappa, he is a Don Juan. Whether or not a Greek really possesses these traits is of little importance to a host of non-Greek individuals. The stereotypic perceptions persist. They may sometimes be confined to a specific geographical region. A Greek organization may have the reputation for being socially oriented in the South while in the Mid-West it may have a reputation for being academically oriented.

A similar association is made between the conventional or non-uniform clothing of Greeks and their Greek affiliation. Because of stereotypes, one Greek organization may be described as being a fashion plate, another as dressing in a drab manner, and another as dressing in a businesslike manner. As a result, a certain image becomes associated with members of a Black Greek sorority or fraternity even when they are "out of uniform."

In addition to contributing to stereotypic perceptions associated with being a Greek, fraternity and sorority membership reveals individual traits of the members. For instance, because Black sororities and fraternities require a solid grade point average of their pledgees, the wearing of colors and symbols of a Greek letter organization communicates to the campus community that one has attained a degree of scholastic success.

Special Activities

The Pledge Period. The pledge period is a time of increased social activity. During this period of initiation, clothing takes on a special meaning for the pledgees. Because they are not yet part of the sorority or fraternity but are still aspiring to become members, their dress is continuously dictated by the Greek organization.

While the pledgees are "on line," as the pledge period is informally called, part of the initiating process dictates that all pledgees dress exactly alike whenever appearing in public as a group. Not only must they dress alike, but they must remain together in a group and walk in a straight line with synchronized movements, often with each carrying a replica of their mascot, be it kitten or elephant or ivy. Each mascot, which represents a virtue, is unique to the sorority or the fraternity.

Fig. 1. The quasi-uniforms of the Omega Psi Phi Fraternity identify group affiliation, yet allow for individuality and flexibility. (Courtesy of Toney McClain)

Fig. 2. The pledgees of the Alpha Phi Alpha Fraternity demonstrate the "cloning of the Greeks." Often during the pledge period, the pledgees are required to dress exactly alike and to remain together in a group, walking with synchronized movements. (Courtesy of Student Activities Office, Howard University)

Fig. 3. Pledgees of the Delta Sigma Theta Sorority participate in a "Step Show." Each sorority's and fraternity's pledgees try to outperform the others as they execute highly creative and original dance steps. (Courtesy of Student Activities Office, Howard University)

The "cloning" of the pledgees serves a dual function: one, it communicates that a pledge group is associated with a particular sorority or fraternity; two, it communicates that the pledgees have not yet acquired full status as sorority or fraternity members. Thus, the pledgees' dress shows both unity and separation, simultaneously.

The visibility of the pledge groups during the initiation period triggers keen competition among the Greeks to have their pledgees appear "most together." "Most together" is translated to mean most fashionably coordinated, most poised, most entertaining and most harmonious and compatible of group. Therefore, special attention is paid to every detail of the pledgees' appearance because it symbolically reflects the degree of "togetherness" experienced by the sorority or fraternity members.

One of the highlights of pledging and one of the most awaited periods on campus is the time when the Greek pledgees perform publicly. These performances are referred to as "Step Shows" or "Stepping" because they involve the coordination and synchronization of intricate, creative, and highly original dance steps. If competition among the Greeks appeared keen before, it becomes intense during the "Step Shows" as each sorority or fraternity tries to outperform the other. Although the competition is lighthearted and fun, no stone is left unturned by each group in the quest for audience applause and consensus that their "step show" performance has been unmatched.

The creativity shown in the dress and adornment of the pledgees during the "step show" is awesome. Often, months before the performance, the sorority and fraternity members make decisions about what the pledgees will be wearing, sometimes employing the services of local seamstresses and designers to create garments that are impressively unique. These garments often have their emblems, symbols, Greek letters and mascots embossed into them. The result is a design, rich in creativity and originality.

While these shows are in progress, the "big sisters or "big brothers" easily stand out in the crowd of viewers because they, too, are bedecked with the sorority's or fraternity's symbols. Especially noteworthy during all of this display is the dying classic, the Greek sweater. The manner in which Black Greeks design their sweaters is no less than a work of art and documented history! The Greek sweater might include one's given name; line number, which is the pledgee's numerical position in line according to height; and line name, which is a special name designated by the "big sisters" or "big brothers" to a pledgee. The line name usually reflects a special trait of the pledgee. Also included on the Greek sweater might be the pledge date, pledge chapter, name of the university where pledged, a full crest of the sorority or fraternity, various Greek symbols and any other statement or slogan that one desires. Each sweater is a one-of-a-kind creation that is sometimes on loan from other Greek members.

During the last week of the initiation period, pledgees may be called probates, a term used to suggest that they are on strict probation. The range of their activities now becomes even more limited than before. In some instances this period is characterized by extremes in clothing and adornment. Pledgees may be seen with garments worn wrong side out and some male pledgees may be seen with haircuts that take on a bizarre quality.

Unlike restrictions dictating their appearance in step shows or as probates, other public performances by Greeks allow more flexibility in type of dress. Sometimes Greeks perform informally "on the block,"—

Fig. 4 and 5. The Classic Greek sweater is a one-of-a-kind creation. It is designed by sorority and fraternity members to be artistic, attractive and an historical document. The sweater pictured in this photograph communicates much about the owner: she is a member of the Delta Sigma Theta Sorority; her name is Aravia; she was number one on her line (indicating that she was the shortest member of her pledge group); her pledge chapter was Beta Epsilon; and she obviously holds her sorority to high esteem as evidenced by the statement, "'That Mighty Delta Band.'" Note also the full crest of the sorority emblazoned on the front of the sweater. (Courtesy of Aravia Holloman)

a designated public area on campus that is easily viewed from many vantage points. These performances may be scheduled or they may be impromptu. Nonetheless, they usually consist of singing songs that exalt the organization's ideals. Because of the more informal nature of such performances, members are allowed to participate even if they are not dressed in symbolic clothing; but it is extremely rare to see a Black Greek performing wearing clothing that does not show his or her group affiliation.

The Mascot as a Clothing Accessory. Reference previously has been made to Black Greek mascots. The importance of mascots needs further clarification.

In the purest sense of the term, a clothing accessory is an item of adornment that is usually worn to complement and enhance one's clothing or body. A mascot is a person, animal, or object adopted by a group as a symbolic figure to bring it good luck. For Black Greeks, their mascot becomes elevated to the status of a clothing accessory, especially for the pledgee. The mascot, carried around by the pledgee for the greater part of the initiation period, becomes part of the total coordinated outfit. Without their mascot, the pledgees' outfit is sometimes incomplete and unacceptable to their big brothers and sisters.

Dress and Rituals. Rituals fall into two broad categories: rites of passage and rites of intensification. Both types of rituals are characterized by an emotional response. A rite of passage is a ceremony that indicates a change of status (Kaiser 430). While this ritual is usually associated with the status of an individual, it can also mark a change in the status of a group. An example of a rite of passage is a birthday party.

A rite of intensification denotes an occasion or event shared by a group or a community of people (Kaiser 430). Rites of intensification evoke a feeling of unity or oneness among the individuals of the group. There is often a response en masse confirming the group's commitment to the event. A Fourth of July celebration is an example of a rite of intensification.

Rites of Passage. Dress plays an important role in the ceremonial rituals of Black Greek letter organizations. During formal rites of passage, dress requirements are often specified in the ritual guidelines. Meticulous compliance to the dress code specified by the ritual demonstrates respect and reverence of the Greeks for their organization. Examples of rites of passage are induction ceremonies and initiation ceremonies. When an undergraduate student goes from being a non-Greek to being a Greek pledgee, the ceremony is laden with symbols of adornment which communicate his or her status. Consequently, there is often a dramatic change in one's wardrobe. As previously recognized, this wardrobe change is a significant mandate. However, in situations where the mandate does not apply, there is continued adherence to this quasi-uniform which suggests great pride in one's newly conferred status.

Once again one observes the notable wardrobe as it becomes even more evident when the Greek pledgee becomes inducted into the sorority or fraternity. The solemn mood of this ceremony is contrasted sharply with the lighthearted mood of the pledge period. Admission into the Greek organization is often symbolically represented by the ceremonious conferring of the sorority's or fraternity's pin. A disappearing ritual is the presentation of the sweater by a Greek family member or friend to the pledgee who has just "crossed," i.e., become fully initiated into the sorority or fraternity. Vestiges of this ritual remain as sorority sisters and fraternity brothers often relinquish their sweaters to the new initiates so that they will be properly clad for their first appearance as full-fledged sorority or fraternity members.

This change in status affords a change in privileges. Therefore, the wearing of specific items of clothing is related to the privileges and responsibilities one is granted by virtue of membership in the organization. Becoming a full Greek member as one relinquishes the pledge status permits the Greek individual to take advantage of resources and to access channels within the organization that the individual could not partake of previously. The newly initiated Greek member can now participate in the ritual of initiating other individuals into the sorority or fraternity. The new Greek usually especially enjoys participating in the initiation ritual at other chapters. Equally enjoyable is accessing additional privileges and resources of other chapters.

For instance, it is well understood by members of the host chapter that the visiting fraternity brother or sorority sister will lodge with them, either in the fraternity or sorority house if one exists, or with individual members in their dorm rooms, homes or apartments.

Another ritual that is accompanied by visible clothing symbols is the selection and the serenading of the sorority or fraternity sweetheart. An informal tradition among Black Greeks is the pairing off of a sorority with a fraternity into what is designated a brother-sister group. Although this trend is changing, the selection of a sweetheart by a Black Greek organization is usually from a member of its brother or sister group. Sororities and fraternities often present their sweethearts with insignia or items of clothing that identify the individual as the group's sweetheart. During the serenading on the block, the sweethearts wear the sweetheart emblem and adorn the colors of the Greek organization that confers the honor upon them.

Rites of Intensification. Like rites of passage, rites of intensification often involve special items of adornment. The Greek Rededication Ceremony is such an example. As the ceremonial title implies, this is a time for recommitting oneself to the goals of the organization. During this ceremony, the members usually wear garments in their colors and their official, formal pin, not the casual pins that have been fashioned to coordinate with casual attire.

Other rites of intensification include fraternity social gatherings that are geographically broader in scope than local campus events. Often these events are regional or national and include large numbers of individuals who have not had previous interaction with each other. Conspicuous symbols of Greek affiliation contribute to their sense of oneness, of commonality of goals, and of similarity of self to others. Thus, clothing plays a part in this informal rite of intensification.

Political Events. Conspicuous displays of clothing and ornamentation are utilized when the sorority or the fraternity is demonstrating civic, community, or political support for a cause. The Greek wardrobe easily identifies group members to the general public. It also shows unity of the group and communicates to the public that the sorority or fraternity is taking a firm stand.

During these events, a deliberate effort is made to clearly identify the group. Therefore, one may wear not only the sweatshirt with the Greek emblems, but may don the hat, pants or skirt, pin, armband, and/or shoes in their Greek colors. They remain in a group and often shout slogans to indicate their position. A newspaper account describes a Black fraternity during a political event:

Wearing the organization's Greek letter symbols on hats, T-shirts and buttons and dressed in the fraternity's colors of purple and gold, the members chanted "Omega Psi Phi says no to apartheid." (Quinn A33)

Additionally, they will likely have printed literature and memorabilia to hand out to the public. As an aside, especially when they are part of masses of people as they are during rallies or marches, they will usually fly a big bunch of balloons high as a signal of location to all their Greek sisters and brothers from various locals who wish to join them.

Summary

Since the inception of the first Black fraternity, Black sororities and fraternities have been quite visible on college campuses due to their conspicuous dress which incorporated much symbolism. Clothing continues to be used symbolically by Black Greeks to communicate nonverbally with the campus community and the larger society. Not only do the clothing symbols communicate Greek affiliation, but they also reveal the stage or level of Greek affiliation, whether pledgee, probate or fully initiated member. The same symbols that communicate group affiliation simultaneously communicate group exclusion, setting the Greeks apart from non-members.

Black sororities and fraternities also use clothing as a quasi-uniform, and in doing so, emphasize the organization or group while suppressing the individuality of the members. Emphasis on the group instead of the members contributes to the formation of stereotypes which result in group labels that may not at all be reflective of traits or tendencies held by individual members.

Finally, clothing symbolism can be seen in the rituals and political activities of Black Greek organizations. In rites of passage, clothing and adornment often symbolize the attainment of a new status. In rites of intensification, clothing and adornment serve to create a sense of unity among the members. Similarly, during political events, Black Greek members use clothing to symbolically indicate their commitment to a cause.

Works Cited

"A Potpourri of Student Concerns: What They're Reading, Wearing, Joining, Applauding, Protesting," *Chronicle of Higher Education* 4 September 1985: 30-2.

"A Sorority Sets New Goals," *New York Times* 28 May 1983, nat'l. ed.: 14.

"Anheuser-Busch Publishes Brochure on Black Greeks," *Jet* Sept. 1985:22.

Appel, Timothy. "US Fraternities: Changing Image Brings on 'Rush'," *The Christian Science Monitor* 28 May 1981: 13.

Bennetts, Leslie. "Ivy League Women Trace Social Barriers," *New York Times* January 1984, nat'l. ed.: 18.

Brooks, Andree. "Greek Row Glows Golden Again," *New York Times* 9 November 1986, nat'l. ed.: 67.

"The Changing Image of College Sororities," *New York Times* 23 January 1984, nat'l. ed.: 18.

Canady, Hortense. "Black Women Leaders: The Case of Delta Sigma Theta," *Urban League Review* Summer 1985: 92-95.

"Canady's National Challenge: Sorority Plans to Aid Single Black Mothers," *Washington Post* 28 January 1984: 81.

Collins, Glenn. "Columbia Fraternities Revive a Rite of Spring," *New York Times* 10 April 1981, nat'l. ed: 28.

Comer, James P. *Beyond Black and White*. New York: Quadrangle Books, 1972.

Ford, Richard. "Rules of the House," *Esquire* June 1986: 231.

"Formation of Fraternities Is On the Increase at Yale," *New York Times* 12 May 1985, nat'l. ed.: 20.

"Fraternities and Sororities: A Dramatic Comeback on Campus," *Ebony* December 1983: 93+.

Greek-Lettered Organizations With An African Heritage. St. Louis: Anheuser-Busch, Inc.

Hechinger, Fred M. "The Fraternities Show Signs of New Strength," *New York Times* 21 May 1985, nat'l. ed.: 13.

Jakobsen, Lyn. "Greek Affiliation and Attitude Change: Developmental Implications," *Journal of College Student Personnel* 27 (1986): 523-27.

Joseph, Nathan. *Uniforms and Nonuniforms Communication Through Clothing.* New York: Greenwood Press, 1986.

Kaiser, Susan B. *The Psychology of Clothing.* New York: Macmillan Publishing Company, 1985.

Keller, Michael J., and Derrell Hart. "The Effects of Sorority and Fraternity Rush on Students' Self Images," *Journal of College Student Personnel,* 23 (1982): 257-61.

King, Pat. "New Wave Networkers," *Black Enterprise* December 1983: 89.

Lord, M.G. "Frats and Sororities: The Greek Rites of Exclusion," *Nation* 4 July 1987: 10+.

Marriott, Michel. "Pioneer's Crusade Goes On: Cofounder Sees Growth of Oldest Black Sorority," *Washington Post* 23 July 1984: D1.

"New Look for Thriving Greeks," *Time* 10 March 1986: 77.

Noble, Jeanne. "A Sense of Place," *Essence* May 1985: 131+.

Quinn, Krystal. "Fraternity Protests Apartheid," *The Washington Post* 31 July 1986: A33.

Roach, Mary Ellen, and Joanne B. Eicher. *The Visible Self: Perspectives on Dress.* Englewood Cliffs: Prentice-Hall Inc., 1973.

Schrager, Rick H. "The Impact of Living Group Social Climate on Student Academic Performance," *Research in Higher Education* 25 (1986): 265-76.

Stemper, William H. (Rev.). "Fraternities, Where Men May Come to Terms With Other Men," Editorial. *New York Times* 16 June 1985: nat'l. ed.: E 20.

Strange, Carney. "Greek Affiliation and Goal of the Academy: A Commentary," *Journal of College Student Personnel* 27 (1986): 519-23.

Wilder, David and Arlyne E. Hoyt. "Greek Affiliation and Attitude Change: A Reply to Jakobsen and Strange," *Journal of College Student Personnel* 27 (1986):527-30.

Wilder, David H., Arlyne E. Hoyt, Beth Shuster Surbeck, Janet C. Wilder and Patricia Imperatrice Carney. "Greek Affiliation and Attitude Change in College Students," *Journal of College Student Personnel* 27 (1986): 510-19.

SORORITY/FRATERNITY	YEAR FOUNDED	CAMPUS FOUNDED	CREST	COLORS	MASCOT
Alpha Phi Alpha Frat.	1906	Cornell Univ.		Black & Gold	None
Alpha Kappa Alpha Soror.	1908	Howard Univ.		Salmon Pink & Apple Green	Ivy
Kappa Alpha Psi Frat.	1911	Indiana Univ.		Crimson & Cream	Shield
Omega Psi Phi Frat.	1911	Howard Univ.		Purple & Gold	None

Chart 1 - Cont'd.

SORORITY/FRATERNITY	YEAR FOUNDED	CAMPUS FOUNDED	CREST	COLORS	MASCOT
Delta Sigma Theta Soror.	1913	Howard Univ.		Crimson & Cream	Duck
Phi Beta Sigma Frat.	1914	Howard Univ.		Royal Blue & White	Dove of Peace
Zeta Phi Beta Soror.	1920	Howard Univ.		Royal Blue & White	Dove of Peace (Official) Kitten (Unofficial)
Sigma Gamma Rho Soror.	1922	Butler Univ.		Blue & Gold	Toy Poodle

All Part of the Act:
A Hundred Years of Costume in
Anglo-American Popular Music

Albert LeBlanc

cos-tume n. 3. A set of clothes appropriate for a particular occasion or season. (*American Heritage Dictionary* 301)

The leading performers of popular music have always been the celebrities of popular culture. Never has their celebrity status been greater than it is today, with their music presented on an almost-continuous basis by the many broadcasters who specialize in popular music, and with their images before the public in settings as varied as televised rock videos and the covers of magazines and tabloids that line the supermarket check out counter.

A crucial part of any popular musician's success is his or her "persona"—an image of personal style for public consumption. Costume is the most important visual ingredient of the persona, and popular musicians rely upon it to develop the image they want to project.

Prominent popular musicians are the leaders, not the followers, in setting the dress styles of the popular culture of their times. It is quite possible that they were not the first individuals to adopt a particular form of dress, but very often they are the people who introduce new styles to the general public because they are the first public figures that a large segment of the public sees wearing a new style. This chapter will describe a century of fashion leadership by prominent performers of popular music.

To the general public, costume may be the most noteworthy and memorable aspect of today's performers of popular music. Musicians tend to invest more money and time in developing their costumes than the average individual invests in a comparable proportion of a wardrobe. In appearance, musicians' costumes are more expensive looking, more trendy, more flashy; and they often have a better fit, though fit is sometimes exaggerated for effect. Musicians' costumes are more humorous, more sexual, more androgynous, more formal, and sometimes even more conservative than the clothes of the general public. In effect, the costume of popular music performers stands out from what the public wears, is noticed by the public, and influences the public. An onlooker doesn't need a musical education to notice and remember how a musician looks.

What is the background over the last hundred years, of the costume of popular music performers? What trends have emerged? What are some of the most noteworthy examples of performer costume during the last century, and how do popular musicians make use of the costumes they wear in advancing their careers and their music? This review will examine these questions, emphasizing musicians' onstage attire rather than what they wear in "everyday life." It is doubtful, in fact, that popular music performers even have an "everyday life" within the contemporary environment of electronic media. The popular musicians of today expect to be noticed and photographed any time they are accessible to the public, and they dress accordingly.

To go back a century in popular music covers a lot of ground— from the time of John Philip Sousa and Scott Joplin to the time of Madonna and Sting. In general, the costumes of popular music performers in 1890 were considerably more conservative than what the norm is today. Minstrel show and vaudeville musicians probably had the most eccentric costumes, if they were performing on stage rather than being hidden in an orchestra pit. But the majority of popular music performers tended to wear a quasi-military band uniform or some version of their Sunday best—a "nice" set of dress clothes.

This period was the heyday of the professional concert band, in both military and civilian versions, and each variety espoused the military form of dress. The United States Marine Band, which Sousa conducted in the 1880's, had a highly elaborate uniform. When Sousa formed his own professional civilian band in 1892, he selected a uniform which was military in style, but which was distinctly more conservative than that worn by the Marine musicians. Nowhere is the change more evident, nor more attractive, than in two famous portraits of Sousa, first as conductor of the Marine Band (Bierley 6) and in his white uniform as leader of his first civilian band (Bierley 13). In *Bands of America*, H. W. Schwartz chronicles the rise and fall of the professional concert bands, and offers many examples of their quasi-military uniforms.

The professional concert bands had their imitators everywhere, and an essential part of the imitation was the uniform. Because many of these imitators were impecunious members of town bands, fraternal organization bands, or just groups of friends who played wind instruments, there was less money available and less pressure to wear a fancy uniform. Even Scott Joplin, the future King of Ragtime, appeared in quasi-military uniform as a member of the Queen City Negro Band in 1896 (Gammond, Plate 26, Page 95). Circus and carnival bands were also much in evidence, and they also tended to wear the quasi-military

Jane Rosemont, Photographer   435 Lathrop, Lansing, MI 48912 (517) 374-7517

"Eric" 1986

uniform. Many of the minstrel show pit bands wore a uniform in the same style.

While the quasi-military uniform was much favored near the end of the last century, it is very likely that the average practitioner of popular music wore some version of his Sunday best to perform. The average popular musician of the day was not a member of a professional concert band, was not involved in vaudeville or minstrelsy, and did not have to keep up with today's tradition of costume notoriety. Al Rose and Edmond Souchon present numerous photographs of the small black bands in and around New Orleans at the turn of the century, and it is a comparatively rare group that appears in uniform. Yet suits, neckties, and hats abound for these, almost exclusively, male musicians. It is evident that many of these performers are low income people wearing their Sunday best. The look of Sunday best can be seen in ragtime and early country music as well as in the earliest groups to perform New Orleans jazz.

What was worn by musicians who made a living playing in bordellos? One might expect these people to approximate the oversexed look of some of today's rock musicians, but that does not seem to be the case.

Most surviving pictures of ragtime musicians show them posing in Sunday best for a formal portrait, or sitting at the keyboard in formal attire with little else in the background. A famous portrait of Tony Jackson shows the celebrated pianist wearing a tuxedo as he sits at his piano (Rose 108). Photographers would not normally be welcome in a bordello, but there is a fascinating picture of the women of one of New Orleans' most elegant houses posing for the camera while Jelly Roll Morton serenades them at the keyboard (Albertson 6-7). Morton appears to be wearing a conservative business suit.

In the hundred years since Sousa became established as a public figure, the costume of popular musicians has become more flamboyant, more sensationalized, and very often more sensual. With many contemporary musicians, the costume worn on stage and electronically transmitted to living rooms across the nation is considerably more sexually provocative than what their musical forebears would have worn to actually perform in a bordello.

Why has costume changed in this way? There have been changes in the underlying culture, with the culture becoming a great deal more liberal. At least equally important is the emergence of new styles of music which did not exist in the last century. Rock music would be the prime example of this. It can be shown that the style of music that is played influences what a performer wears more strongly than anything else.

A study of performer costume may safely begin with the clothing that is worn, including color, pattern, material, adornment, fit, accessories, and manner of wearing all of the above. Especially in the case of rock musicians, any study of clothing must also survey that which is not worn.

In the area of color, Deborah Harry's wearing of black (Harry, Stein, and Bockris 35) greatly influenced the punk rock subculture of the late seventies, and Tanya Tucker's bright red jump suit worn for an album cover in 1978 (Polhemus and Procter 65) signalled a shift to a more adventurous persona. Color is extensively used by even the most conservative performers of country music to enhance their stage presence. Sometimes color has been used as a personal trademark, for example by country singer Johnny Cash, nicknamed The Man in Black (Carr 258). Cash embraced the color black long before it became fashionable in the late seventies and early eighties. Popular musicians have not been reticent in their use of color, often wearing striking hues which members of the general public would not dare put on.

Pattern has also served popular musicians well. Bill Haley's plaid and printed sport coats gave an upbeat appearance to his band (White 89), while paisley prints served to tie musicians into the styles of the psychedelic era. Animal coat prints, such as imitation leopard skin (Polhemus and Procter 48) tiger skin, and even zebra (Harry, Stein, and

Bockris 34) have been popular with both male and female rock performers. Rock singer Deborah Harry has used the animal skin look extensively in developing her persona.

Visually striking material has often been used to make performer garments. An often-cited example of this would be Elvis Presley's gold lame suit of the 1950s (Torgoff 195), but the field also includes black leather worn with elan by Elvis and Jim Morrison in the sixties, the rhinestones especially favored by country musicians; sequins, spandex, rubber, plastic, gauze, velveteen, and other unusual materials too numerous to mention (see Polhemus and Procter).

Perhaps the most memorable use of black leather was made by Elvis Presley when he wore a complete suit of it in his televised comeback special of 1968 (Goldman 290). Jim Morrison of The Doors used a rather standard (for rock musicians) black leather suit early in his career (Sugerman 37), but shifted to a gray leather which gave a strong reptilian effect (Sugerman 146), perhaps intended as a tie-in with the "Ceremony of the Lizard" used in his stage act.

A standard approach to costume notoriety has been to start with a striking fabric in a striking color and a striking cut, and add ornamentation, usually with some combination of rhinestones and sequins. Aging country musicians of the most conservative lifestyle have dropped all vestiges of conservatism in their own efforts to develop memorable costumes. Hank Snow and Porter Wagoner (Strobel 106, 115) typify this approach, though Elvis Presley in his later years equalled them for rhinestone-studded splendor (Torgoff 218-19). A typically flamboyant Hank Snow costume is on exhibit at Nashville's Country Music Hall of Fame and Museum. While he was not considered a practitioner of country music, the late pianist Liberace had a healthy appetite for rhinestone encrusted costumes (Polhemus and Procter 95). Among the younger generation, Michael Jackson is making sure that the rhinestone tradition survives.

Blue denim served as the uniform of the rock culture, and rock idol Bruce Springsteen appeals to its historical roots by wearing a pair of ancient red tag Levi's in a cut that was popular in the fifties (Dean and Howells 195). It is probably no accident that red tag Levi's in the same cut and featuring the venerable button-up fly sold very well in the mid-eighties as Springsteen's popularity soared.

Fit is one aspect of costume in which popular music performers have often departed from public norms while also influencing the evolution of style. As might be expected, fit has run the entire gamut from very loose to very tight. Band leaders Cab Calloway and Louis Jordan helped to popularize the loose fitting men's zoot suit of the forties, and this garb enjoyed a British comeback during the rock era (Polhemus and Procter 113). Liberace has appeared in capes of magnificent expansiveness, and some of the most outrageously attired punk and heavy metal rock bands have used capes to create a contrast with costumes which are either skin tight or very largely missing (Polhemus and Procter 20-21).

Tight fitting clothes became a virtual uniform of the rock culture during the seventies, though they were strongly in evidence both before and after that decade. An early classic example was the very fitted leather jeans worn by Jim Morrison early in his career (Sugerman 37, 83), but their tightness was soon eclipsed by creations of the seventies, as exemplified by Rod Stewart's imitation leopard skin tights (White 184-85) and Tanya Tucker's jump suit worn for the cover of her "TNT" album of 1978 (Polhemus and Procter 65). Other musicians carried the trend to what must have been its limits (Polhemus and Procter 126-27).

Accessories have always been an easy way to personalize one's dress style, and popular musicians have not overlooked this opportunity. For years they have used hats, gloves, scarves, and various other artifacts to express an individualistic way of dressing.

Hats are one of the most widely used fashion accessories in popular music, and who could quickly forget Bob Wills' cowboy hat worn to front his Western swing band (Townsend 271), Thelonius Monk's beret which became an emblem of bebop jazz in its infancy (Gottlieb 115), or Frank Sinatra's mainstream hat (Howlett 80) which became such a recognizable part of his image in the fifties? The most famous hat in American popular music may be Cousin Minnie Pearl's flowery straw hat with its prominent attached price tag, worn for years on broadcasts of the Grand Ole Opry (Hurst 163).

Gloves have not been overlooked in the quest of popular musicians for a distinctive appearance. Sousa launched his return to civilian life after World War I by ordering one hundred dozen pairs of white calfskin gloves, to be used in conducting his professional concert band (Schwartz 284-85). Bierley maintains that Sousa's conducting gloves were made of kid rather than calfskin, and offers a photo (Bierley 134). Michael Jackson is a famous contemporary wearer of gloves. He is known for cutting off the fingertips, adding a great many sequins, and he often wears only one glove for additional accent.

Artifacts that distinguish specific performers would include such things as Bob Wills' cigar, which was as famous as his hat (Bob Wills *King of Western Swing* cover). Sousa was quoted as admiring the company of a good cigar more than most other creature comforts, and he made them a part of his style by having his favorite brand prepared with a drawing of himself on the wrapper (Bierley 102). It is reported that the origin of Rudy Vallee's megaphone was the singer's weak voice, but the resulting visual trademark stood him in good stead when he appeared in print media (Simon, *Best of the Music Makers* 583).

The manner of wearing accessories has been almost as important as the accessories themselves in creating a memorable image for a performer. Frank Sinatra's hats were usually a standard menswear product, but he wore them at a jaunty angle, often far back on his head (Howlett 65, 87, 107), but sometimes far down over his brow (Howlett 95). Deborah Harry of Blondie wore a standard pair of tight fit Levi jeans. What was different was the fact that they were badly torn (Harry, Stein, and Bockris 132). In 1987, teenagers paid a premium price for worn and torn jeans bought new in a shopping mall. The different thing about Cousin Minnie Pearl's hat was its prominently displayed price tag.

It is probably fair to say that the clothing which is not worn has led to as much costume notoriety among popular musicians as that which is worn. Varying degrees of undress also make a costume statement. Elvis Presley contributed to a male dress style trend of many years running by simply leaving an extra button undone below the collar of his shirt. Elvis' single open buttonhole (Torgoff 135) soon became two (Torgoff 94), and near the end of his life the open gap approached his expanding waistline (Goldman 290). The look depended upon the absence of an undershirt, and it flourished thus during the sixties and seventies, worn mainly by rock and disco performers and their audiences. Much to the relief of undershirt manufacturers, the men's open shirt look of the middle and late eighties came to reveal a brightly colored tank top rather than bare skin.

As rock music matured, levels of male undress escalated. Singer Jim Morrison was merchandised as a sex symbol, a persona he carefully cultivated in 1967, asking a Hollywood hair stylist to shape his mane like that observed on a statue of Alexander the Great (Hopkins and Sugerman 144), and posing shirtless for photo sessions with *16* and *Vogue* magazines and for Elektra Records photographer Joel Brodsky. Judging from the frequency with which they have been reprinted, Brodsky's photos of the shirtless Morrison were a visual bonanza for Elektra, and one of them became known as the "Young Lion" shot (Hopkins and Sugerman 156; see cover of the same book or Sugerman 33 for photo). Mick Jagger (White front cover), Iggy Pop (Logan and Woffinden 184), and Ted Nugent (Ellis 134) all made shirtless performance a part of their style. Iggy Pop's shirtless condition gave his audience a better view of his blood when he chose to cut himself as part of his stage act.

While male musicians were shedding their shirts, some of their female counterparts were getting rid of their bras, and making sure that their audiences noticed the results. Punk rocker Patti Smith wore the braless look on the cover of her Easter album (Patti Smith Group) and assumed a pose in which she appeared to be looking down at her own tank top. The irrepressible Debbie Harry went braless often (Harry, Stein, and Bockris 99), and women performers in music styles other than rock also espoused this look in the seventies, for example folk singers Kate and Anna McGarrigle (Baggelaar and Milton 283), country rock singer Rita Coolidge (Dellar and Thompson 58), and soul singer Chaka Kahn (Futrell et al. 163).

While male rock musicians have sometimes removed clothing in a performance, female rockers have occasionally worn see-through garments in concert. Rose Simpson of the Incredible String Band wore a see-through dress of sheer white gauze to perform at the Woodstock festival (Young and Lang 58), and Linda Ronstadt wore a similar but less revealing dress for one of her album covers (Russell 236). Diana Ross (White 191), Claudia Barry (Polhemus and Procter 106), and Deborah Harry (Bangs 73) were other female performers who embraced the see-through look of the late sixties and seventies.

A female bare chested look was suggested by the symbolism of one of Madonna's costumes for her "Who's That Girl" tour of 1987. Over the breast section of an opaque black garment in the style of a corset, the pop star wore glossy imitation nipples of bright copper color (Elias 13). At one point in the act, black tassels were suspended from the tops of the ornaments (Elias 31). Madonna looked conservative compared to punk rocker Wendy O. Williams, who wore similar but more exaggerated ornaments (Polhemus and Procter 107). The difference was that Williams wore them over bare skin, a decision which may have contributed to her arrest for indecent exposure (Polhemus and Procter 83).

The ultimate female breast baring of the sixties came from a performer who was not even engaged in popular music. Classical cellist Charlotte Moorman established a reputation for various forms of nudity in her performances, with her first topless concert in New York City leading to her arrest in mid-recital and earning her the night in jail. Her unique approach to the traditions of art music was more successful in Europe, where she completed without arrest a performance in which movie cartoons were projected on her nude body while she sat astride a metal "bomb" and bowed it with a saw (*The Instrumentalist* Nov. 1968, 10).

Wendy O. Williams and Charlotte Moorman were hardly alone among musicians in being arrested for indecent exposure. A highly celebrated case was Jim Morrison's arrest, but Morrison chalked up the added notoriety of being charged with "lewd and lascivious behavior" for a 1969 performance in Miami (Hopkins and Sugerman 236, 238).

Rock performer nudity, originally espoused with an eye toward occasional sexual excitement, came to be an overworked convention which could leave the jaded beholder with an impression of general tastelessness. Many of the open shirted males in Robert Ellis's *Pictorial Album of*

Rock are in a state of physical development which would look better covered up. The Tubes' extreme of nudity and attempted sexuality (Ellis 204-05) shows how far some rock groups were willing to go.

The category of performer grooming involves hair style, including facial hair, fingernails, and use of makeup. Hair style can become an easily recognizable trademark, and some classics in this area were the tenderly boyish bangs of the early period Beatles (Logan and Woffinden 27), Bill Haley's famous spit curl (Logan and Woffinden 101), and Little Richard's rampant pompadour (Palmer 220-21). Earlier eras saw the slicked down look of Paul Whiteman and Bix Beiderbecke. Total baldness has always made a strong visual effect, and early jazz man King Oliver and latter day soul man Isaac Hayes (Futrell et al. 152, Polhemus and Procter 104) wore the look with elan. Oliver's baldness gave him a special poignant dignity (Rose 119).

Some performers have changed the color of their hair for visual effect. Deborah Harry is a natural brunette (Bangs 55), but began a ritual of routine bleaching of her hair to front the rock group Blondie (Bangs 53). At one point she used peroxide to render it silvery white for the production of a picture disc (Polhemus and Procter 86).

Eyebrows can be present or absent, and accentuated or not. Light but geometric eyebrows are essential to the look of Annie Lennox of The Eurhythmics (Lennox and Stewart 28-29). Eyebrow geometry is also essential to Boy George (Polhemus and Procter 78). Lennox uses eye shadow makeup as an important part of her overall look, and male performers Michael Jackson and David Bowie use eye shadow as much as do women.

Moustaches offer male musicians an opportunity for a distinctive facial look, and this look has ranged from the pencil-thin moustache of dapper society band leader Shep Fields (Simon *Simon Says* 65), through the slightly heavier versions worn by Paul Whiteman (Walker 423), the young Duke Ellington (Dance frontispiece), and Bix Beiderbecke (Prendergast 31), to the full grown drooping moustache worn by Frank Zappa (Ellis 222-23).

Sideburns became an Elvis Presley trademark fairly early in his public life, and he sported a stylish pair for the filming of his 1968 television special. Unfortunately they kept expanding and seemed almost parodistic near the end of his life (Goldman 290).

Male performers have used beards to attain a wide variety of looks. It is especially fascinating to note a progression of bearded looks on the same performer, and Jim Morrison may be the best example because of his very short public life. As a young sex symbol, Morrison was clean shaven (Lisciandro inside cover). As he turned to blues in his musical style he dropped his slinky costumes in favor of a white T-shirt and blue denim. Meanwhile, he grew a full beard (Lisciandro 70). His beard continued to develop into a long, curly, guru look (Lisciandro 89, 157-58). In short, the beard fit the persona. For his trial in federal court for obstructing the duties of an airline flight crew, the usually-scruffy Morrison appeared clean shaven wearing a blazer and necktie.

Long a target of patronizing commercials, the dusky precursor of male beard formerly known as five o'clock shadow has enjoyed unprecedented acclaim in the eighties. While some have hypothesized that it cost Richard Nixon at least one election, it has become an indicator of male coolness after its favorable introduction to the public on the successful television series "Miami Vice." Jim Morrison was actually one of its pioneers (Lisciandro 6), but it took popular contemporaries such as Sting (*Creem Rock Shots* 18) to get the look better established among musicians. George Michael and Jon Bon Jovi are two of the newer performers to wear the look (*Creem Rock Shots* 67, 51).

If Sting typifies the currently popular shadow-beard look, country musician Kenny Rogers is a good example of the more traditional beard—fuller and longer, but very neatly trimmed (Dellar and Thompson 200). Rock musicians Ian Anderson of Jethro Tull, Jerry Garcia of the Grateful Dead, and Billy Gibbons and Dusty Hill of ZZ Top have modeled some the longest and fullest beards in popular music (Ellis 111, 102; Polhemus and Procter 137).

The color of a beard can also convey a message. Sousa's dark full beard worn when he assumed command of the U.S. Marine Band gave an impression of youth as well as authority. On the other hand, the gray of Kenny Rogers' beard speaks of maturity and experience, and this impression also surfaces sometimes in the lyrics of his songs. There is something of a graybeard tradition in country music, with recurrent admonitions that one had better show respect for a graybeard.

Makeup is an aspect of grooming which is associated almost exclusively with females by the general public. This is not the case with performers, who all need some of it to avoid a deathly pallor under the intensity of stage or television lighting. Rock musicians, however, have hardly stopped at the moderate amounts of makeup needed to ward off pallor. During the glitter rock era of the seventies, David Bowie wore stabbing streaks of makeup across his face in the shape of a lightning bolt (Polhemus and Procter 75). By the end of the decade, Kiss had established a painted-face look which made Bowie seem conservative (Polhemus and Procter 77, Ellis 120). At that point in their career, the members of Kiss so valued the look that they refused to be interviewed or photographed without full makeup.

For many people eyeglasses are merely a necessity for seeing, but popular music performers have even turned their mundane spectacles into personal trademarks. Pince nez glasses were a Sousa trademark (Bierley 83), while Benny Goodman and Glenn Miller wore wire rim models which were almost frameless (Simon *Simon Says* 48, 433). Buddy Holly could be recognized by his black plastic eyeglass frames, and it would appear that he and Roy Orbison must have gone to the same optician (Polhemus and Procter 50). Blind musician Ray Charles has dark glasses in frames similar to Holly's. For him they have become a timeless and very personal trademark (White 49).

In the sixties, John Lennon espoused wire rim frames which contrasted with the plastic frames of the fifties, and Grace Slick performed at the Woodstock Festival in rose tinted wire rim octagons (Young and Lang 63). The glasses which Janis Joplin wore at Woodstock were tinted orange and quite oversize in contrast to Slick's (Young and Lang 62). Among contemporary performers, eyewear styles have ranged from the Ben Franklin frames worn by country musician Grandpa Jones (Hurst 145) through the very highly styled plastic frames favored by Elton John (Ellis 113).

Musicians have generally remained close to the trends of their times in selection of eyewear, but sometimes they are responsible for creating new trends. It would require methodical historical investigation to determine whether they created a style or helped to popularize a style which had been originated by others.

Jewelry is a standard means of personal adornment, and popular musicians of both sexes have made ample use of it. Liberace may be the classic example, but Elvis Presley and Jim Morrison used it to good effect in designing their own looks. One of the most striking uses of jewelry has been made by soul performer Isaac Hayes, who has often appeared shirtless wearing very heavy gold chains arranged in a way reminiscent of suspenders (Futrell et al, 119, 152). Jelly Roll Morton had a front tooth which displayed a diamond embedded in gold (Albertson 26). Sadly, he had to pawn this famous ornament for living expenses near the end of his life.

The tatoo is another form of personal adornment which has been used by musicians. Actress-musician Cher may have the most famous tatoo in popular music. It is located on her buttock, and she has worn costumes which display it (*People Weekly*, January 14, 1980, 63).

In summary, what uses have popular music performers made of costume? They have used it to define a persona. They have used it to differentiate roles within a group, and these roles have been as varied as band leader, sideman, clown, or sex object. They have used costume to create and maintain a specific personal trademark. They have used costume to stay up to date, always remaining stylish and current. Some have decided not to stay up to date, instead giving the public another view of styles which have already proven to be popular. Many have used costume to show unanimity with the conventions of a musical style. Others have used costume to defy convention and create outrage, saying that they are only doing what the public really wants to do but doesn't dare.

For its own part, what has been the public's reaction to the costume of popular music performers? Sometimes the public denounces it, sometimes the public imitates it, but always the public notices it. And that is what performers want more than anything else.

Works Cited

Albertson, Chris. *Jelly Roll Morton*. Giants of Jazz Series. Alexandria, VA: Time-Life Records, 1979.

American Heritage Dictionary of the English Language. Ed. William Morris. Boston: Houghton Mifflin, 1969.

Baggelaar, Kristin, and Donald Milton. *Folk Music: More Than a Song*. New York: Crowell, 1976.

Bangs, Lester. *Blondie*. New York: Simon and Schuster, 1980.

Bierley, Paul E. *John Philip Sousa: American Phenomenon*. Englewood Cliffs, NJ: Prentice-Hall, 1973.

Carr, Patrick. Ed. *The Illustrated History of Country Music*. Garden City, NY: Doubleday, 1979.

Creem Rock Shots. March, 1988.

Dance, Stanley. *Duke Ellington*. Giants of Jazz Series. Alexandria, VA: Time-Life Records, 1978.

Dean, Roger, and David Howells. *The Ultimate Album Cover Album*. New York: Prentice Hall, 1987.

Dellar, Fred, and Roy Thompson. *The Illustrated Encyclopedia of Country Music*. New York: Harmony, 1977.

Elias, Rich. "Madonna Live." *Rock Scene Presents Concert Shots*. March, 1988: 12+.

Ellis, Robert. *The Pictoral Album of Rock*. New York: Crescent, 1981.

Futrell, Jon, et al. *The Illustrated Encyclopedia of Black Music*. New York: Harmony, 1982.

Gammond, Peter. *Scott Joplin and the Ragtime Era*. New York: St. Martin's Press, 1975.

Goldman, Albert. *Elvis*. New York: McGraw-Hill, 1981.

Gottlieb, William P. *The Golden Age of Jazz*. New York: Simon and Schuster, 1979.

Harry, Debbie, Chris Stein, and Victor Bockris. *Making Tracks: The Rise of Blondie*. New York: Dell, 1982.

Hopkins, Jerry, and Danny Sugerman. *No One Here Gets Out Alive*. New York: Warner, 1980.

Howlett, John. *Frank Sinatra*. New York: Simon and Schuster, 1979.

Hurst, Jack. *Nashville's Grand Ole Opry*. New York: Abrams, 1975.

Lennox, Annie, and Dave Stewart. *Eurhythmics in Their Own Words*. Sydney, Australia: Omnibus, 1984.

Lisciandro, Frank. *Jim Morrison: An Hour for Magic*. New York: Delilah, 1982.

Logan, Nick, and Bob Woffinden. *The Illustrated Encyclopedia of Rock*. New York: Harmony, 1977.

Patti Smith Group. *Easter*. Arista 4171, 1978.

Palmer, Tony. *All You Need is Love*. Hammondsworth, England: Penguin, 1977.

People Weekly, "Cher's Bottom Line," 14 Jan. 1980: 63.

Polhemus, Ted, and Lynn Procter. *Pop Styles.* London: Vermilion, 1984.

Prendergast, Curtis. *Bix Beiderbecke.* Giants of Jazz Series. Alexandria, VA: Time-Life Records, 1979.

Rose, Al. *Storyville, New Orleans.* University, AL: U. of Alabama Press, 1974.

Rose, Al, and Edmond Souchon. *New Orleans Jazz.* Rev. ed. Baton Rouge: Louisiana State UP, 1978.

Russell, Ethan A. *Dear Mr. Fantasy.* Boston: Houghton Mifflin, 1985.

Schwartz, H. W. *Bands of America.* Garden City, NY: Doubleday, 1957.

Simon, George T. *Simon Says: The Sights and Sounds of the Swing Era 1935-1955.* New Rochelle, NY: Arlington House, 1971.

Simon, George T. *The Best of the Music Makers.* Garden City, NY: Doubleday, 1979.

Strobel, Jerry. Ed. *Grand Ole Opry: WSM Picture-History Book.* Nashville, TN: WSM, 1976.

Sugerman, Danny. *The Doors: The Illustrated History.* New York: William Morrow, 1983.

The Instrumentalist. "A Unique Cello Recital," Nov. 1968: 10

Torgoff, Martin, Ed. *The Complete Elvis.* New York: Delilah, 1982.

Townsend, Charles R.*San Antonio Rose: The Life and Music of Bob Wills.* Urbana, IL: U. of Illinois Press, 1976.

Walker, Leo. *The Big Band Almanac.* Pasadena, CA: Ward Richie, 1978.

White, Timothy. *Rock Stars.* New York: Stewart, Tabori, & Chang, 1984.

Wills, Bob. *King of Western Swing.* MCA-543, 1973.

Young, Jean, and Michael Lang. *Woodstock Festival Remembered.* New York: Ballantine, 1979.

Punks

Barbara K. Nordquist

Black leather jacket studded with metal rivets, black, torn old trousers or short black skirt, five earrings including a safety pin in the ear, gloves without fingers, shockingly colored hair in "spikes" on top of the head— this is a typical description of a *punk* as seen in American society today. While some onlookers reel in horror, others even copy aspects of the dress which they may have at first abhorred. Who are these punks and why has a "fad" which started over fifteen years ago continued to attract converts today in spite of numerous distasteful events surrounding them?

The answers to these questions are complex. Dr. Rex Beaber of the UCLA Medical School notes that at "any given time in history, there's always been a percentage of young people who are nihilistic, despairing, with psychological disorders and into a lot of drug use" (Conklin). Punk "embodies the dementia of a nihilistic generation," according to the narrator in *Sid and Nancy*, the 1986 film about Sid Vicious, the "Sex Pistols" punk bass player who died of a drug overdose in 1979. Yet others see the punk dress and life style as a simple expression of teenage uniqueness and eagerness to present "oneself" differently from the previous generation and one's peers.

The threat of this punk phenomenon was perceived as so great that a seminar with 150 participants was held on the subject in Pasadena, California in May, 1985. Participants included parents, psychiatrists and police who discussed "the potentially evil effects of the punk and heavy metal cultures." The conference sponsors were two former Orange County probation officers who saw a link between the aggressive music and lifestyle (including clothes) and self inflicted wounds, homicide and suicide in the punk sub culture.

Some punks, however, denied that their behavior reflected these tendencies; they believed in anti-vivisectionism and peace. A few young people even turned the phenomenon into profit-making businesses. Drew, age 24, developed and manufactured punk rock-inspired "intense street fashions" for his two year old company *Lip Service* (Leven, 31). When Stephen Sprouse opened a 5600 square foot SoHo boutique in September, 1987, he unabashedly promoted 1970s punk rock inspired clothing. He and his backers hoped for a continued interest and growth in this counter-culture inspired fashion and planned to open more stores should the interest hold (Gross 6).

What then is the punk style? What clothing styles does it encompass and how does it continue to have appeal when other fads have long since faded? What is its draw and continuing hold on young people?

Clothing Style Origin

Punk clothing was launched as a fashion statement in the early 1970s by Vivienne Westwood, an avant-garde British clothing designer (Sones). In 1986, she said that the movement was dead and moved on to the "crini" look, short skirts with hoops inspired by Minnie Mouse. She was the "high priestess" of punk when she and her partner, Malcolm McLaren, also a punk-rock producer, launched *Let it rock,* a successful boutique on London's Kings' Road in 1971. Her fashions were "street" fashions rooted in anti-establishment behavior seen in safety pins through the cheeks and similar self-mutilating expressions. The link between fashion and music was a major point she made. This link continues today.

These London fashions soon skipped the Atlantic to New York, Los Angeles, and Washington, D.C. In no time punk rockers were found everywhere, in small and large towns. Their clothes were meant to express a rebellious lifestyle.

Source of Clothing

Innovative clothing suppliers quickly filled the new demand for old, cast off, mostly black clothing. Used clothing stores such as those sponsored by the Salvation Army, Purple Heart Society and Goodwill supplied many of the punk rockers needs (Hirshey 38). Street vendors, who solicited sales of specialized punk rockers accessories, also soon set up their carts. Metal-studded belts, black T-shirts, and earrings, were *de rigeur.* These essential punk items and items specifically made for the punk rockers, were sold not only by the street vendors, but also by the newly established fashion shops. The punks also bartered for these items between themselves. The black leather metal-studded jacket became the most desired punk item of clothing. This jacket was, no doubt, a holdover from the "motorcycle gang uniform" which has endured as a subculture fashion item for decades. The jackets, available because of their use by motorcycle groups, were found at rummage stores or supplied by street vendors. However, their high cost required family, job or drug money for purchase (Mason 1). Seemingly this was not an insurmountable problem for most punks found ways to get the money needed (Laws 5).

The longevity of the punk style contributed to the aforementioned business venture of Stephen Sprouse in New York City. Fall 1987 was the opening date for his punk-inspired shop with safety-pin studded shirts, eleven-inch-long mini skirts in olive drab melton and Day-Glo and colored flannel suits. Since the punk style began in 1971 all of these styles had been seen before but the appeal apparently had not faded, at least that is what Sprouse's backers, GFI/Knoll International Holdings, who financed his venture, believed. Sprouse intended to combine punk inspired styles with "generic" core designers and to price the whole line within reach of the young. To achieve this end he divided his shop into three floors. Each floor progressively provided better quality and therefore more expensive merchandise. The ground floor had Stephen Sprouse labeled garments such as the now familiar motorcycle jacket for $150. On the middle floor, the motorcycle jacket in wool melton sold for $350 while on the top floor the jackets cost over $1,000 (Gross 6).

Sprouse was running against the trend for Westwood and other punk designers have moved on to other styles. But was he right and were they wrong? Did punk clothing move from fad to fashion? Has the punk-counter-culture movement become a permanent subculture among the young? The need for an outlet for those nihilistic youth has not vanished and the clothing as a visible symbol of their despair is still seen on the streets of America. Commander Salamander, a boutique in Georgetown, D.C. with an excess of one million per year in sales, offers an eclectic mix of avant-garde and the shocking. Similar business successes are found across the country (Lewis 15).

Clothing Styles

The 1986 film *Sid and Nancy* about the "Sex Pistols" bass player, Sid Vicious and his American girlfriend, Nancy, is a permanently recorded visual source of the clothing styles of the 1970s punk rocker. Sid Vicious died of a drug overdose in 1979 and the movie relates portions of his life with his girlfriend prior to his death.

In the film, Sid and his friends wore black jeans or trousers or leather jeans, torn T-shirts, black metal-studded leather jackets, gun belts, leather gloves without fingers, and leather neck bands studded with metal. Nancy and her friends wore black clothing also, the gloves, leather jackets, belts and neckbands corresponding to the male clothing but instead of jeans the females wore tight, short skirts in black leather or fabric with fishnet stockings and high heels. The women whitened their skin and used heavy makeup to outline and highlight their eyes and lips.

The hair styles depicted in the movie were the most noteworthy part of the costume. Hair was often dyed coal black and teased to stand straight out from the head. Sometimes bleached blond hair was seen, but perhaps the most shocking effect came from neon-orange, green and blue hair, the quintessential symbol of the punk rocker. This was achieved by first bleaching the hair and then coloring it. Another equally popular hair style was the cut called the "mohawk." The style was given this name because it was thought to look similar to that worn by the Mohawk Indians. The desired look is achieved by shaving two to three inches of hair from the sides of the head leaving a two to three inch fringe extending from the forehead to the nape of neck. A long piece of hair may be left hanging down the back to add a dramatic ending. This fringe may be dyed black, bleached blonde or bleached and colored. The outrageous hair in the film, as well as in the real lives of punks is the "crowning glory" of the punk rockers and perhaps the most revealing statement they try to make about their nihilistic view of life. Their punk hair styles often make it difficult for the rocker to find work in conventional establishments, even a job at McDonald's would be impossible with such hair styles. Rockers must make money in some other way.

Other snubs to "regular society" are followed by punk rockers as well. In one final scene of *Sid and Nancy*, Sid is dressed in a white tuxedo jacket, jeans, boots and no shirt. Nancy is in an old wedding dress, a crown of thorns and pounds of rhinestones. This statement about the duplicity and inconsistency in the customs and conventions of straight society are hard to miss. In this scene the punks profane the sacred in an affront to the Christian wedding ceremony by wearing symbols of purity and chastity, festivity and joyousness in combination with the ultimate symbol of unselfish love, the crown of thorns. They are pointing out that these symbols have become mere fashion images, without real meaning. They believe that people who continue to use them seriously leave themselves open to laughter and ridicule. Fashion is seen as ridiculous to punk rockers, even though they too slavishly follow set clothing styles to clearly identify themselves as punks.

According to British designer Katherine Hammett, the early punk sub culture in Britain was composed largely of working class youth who were frustrated at not being able to advance beyond their class. She felt British society placed little value on the young and thus being ignored, they decided to rebel by making a bold statement in their clothing choice. American children, perhaps, have the opposite problem. Too much attention may be lavished on them. Therefore, their reasons for choosing clothing non-conformity becomes one of untying the apron strings and achieving an independent identity. Whatever the reasons for the beginnings of the punk's unique styles, the daring innovations breaking with the traditional mode injected an energy in clothing design which has been transferred to the general population. Punk styles have been widely copied by the rest of society but usually in more subdued form.

"Punk" by Nicole Barrick

Fig. 1

Fig. 2

Fig. 3

Figs. 1, 2 & 3.
Punks in Georgetown (Washington, D.C.)
Photos by Silvy Nordquist

Fig. 4.
Punk in Bethesda, Maryland
Photo by Silvy Nordquist

While punk may no longer be common place in Kings' Road in London, it was still avant-garde in the suburbs of Washington, D.C. in 1987. And street fashion remains a source of inspiration for many conventional American designers.

Analysis

Clothing is used in our society in many ways but perhaps the most compelling reason for its use by punk rockers is as a symbol of their feeling of separation from and rejection by normal society. The extreme edge to which these youth push acceptability in body covering is evident in the nonconformist styles they wear. To understand a communicating symbol, we, as observers, need to have a shared meaning with the wearers about the symbols they are expressing. Most of us simply do not share the punk lifestyle and therefore cannot accurately interpret their symbols and fail to comprehend the message they are broadcasting. Our actions towards these youth are based on our own beliefs and values. Women therefore assign meanings which are perhaps not the same as those meant by the punks. The wedding dress with crown of thorns worn by Nancy in the movie *Sid and Nancy* evokes a very picturesque symbolic meaning to those of us in mainline society. The combination of the two is so bizarre that we can only deduce that the wearer is mocking all that is sacred to the rest of us.

The different backgrounds and experiences of people in mainline society and those of the punks, especially punk rockers, makes it difficult for many people to interpret punk clothing symbols. But, then, what is so unusual about the backgrounds of the punks that leads them to adopt different clothing styles from the rest of society? Perhaps as some English authors have suggested, it is the rejection of their own importance as teens that causes the rebellion. The psychiatrists may be right in writing that a certain number of teens will always reject society's norms and look for a radical group to join. The radical subculture of the 1970s and 1980s is the punk new wave group. Perhaps rejection of conventional culture is the common background that binds them together.

"The Life of a Punk," by Mike Sager in the *Washingtonian Magazine* (181) describes in vivid detail the social interaction process of the punks on Dupont Circle in Washington, D.C. Greg and Kitty were raised in suburban families. Kitty attended an exclusive girls school before leaving her "parental imposed" life to go her own way. Punks like Greg and Kitty live in filthy apartments, filled with trash and rodents and friends. They bum money, get menial jobs where their clothing and hair styles will not offend (or frighten) the public, or they deal in drugs. Occasionally they get money, a good nights' rest and a shower from a "poseur," kids from the suburbs who dress like punks and hang around them at the Circle but go back home at night. The "poseurs" have learned the symbols;

they can interact with the punks because they have learned the language and meanings of their style of dress. They are not, however, willing to accept the unhealthy and dangerous lifestyle of the full-time punk. Some would say they are wise to retreat to the safety of their homes at night.

The meanings assigned to clothing are modified over time; the interpretations vary as the symbols change. Society gives meaning to a symbol based upon its tradition, use and culture. Thus, the punk's safety pin through the cheek shocks the typical observer because the symbolic use and meaning of a safety pin has nothing to do with self-mutilation. Indeed, it is meant to protect the body, and is often associated with harmless babies. A more dramatic twisting of the symbolic meaning of an object is hard to imagine.

While the symbolic meaning of the various clothing styles the punks wear may be unclear to us, the observers, the "right clothes" as symbols of the punk style are usually clear to the punks themselves. But the "dress code" required of a punk can get to be too much for even a truly rebellious youth. This was aptly expressed by "Jake," a 27 year old punk, who commented as follows about the changing "scene" on DuPont Circle over a period of eleven years:

It's like the new kids, like, there's nothing about politics anymore, sad to say. It used to be that way. It was naive and idealistic in a way, but I mean, we thought we could change something. It was no organized protest as such. You didn't have to protest. You just walked around, and you were a symbol for what you were trying to say, whatever it was. I mean, it wasn't—I mean, now people have really turned into this kind of bad joke in a way. You got to have the right clothes, the right this, the right that. (Sager 188)

The latest symbol to fall to the punk rockers' beat is the polka. Made a symbol of squareness by Laurence Welk, the traditional polka styles of dress were taken up by a group of New York women and West Coast men who dressed in studded lederhosen or black skirts of varying lengths, bar-room bare tops, and fish net hose. They played a hybrid combination of polka and punk rock music (*People Magazine* 69). Thus searching to destroy symbols of respectability, these groups have discovered yet another middle-age politeness to mock. They seem to scream: "look how we can turn your icons to silly symbols."

Conclusion

During the Fall of 1987, ABC aired an after school special, "The Day My Kid Went Punk," which featured a dramatic confrontation between a parent and a teen-age child over a value system struggle ("Day My Kid..."). The child/man wants to be noticed, the parent wants a "normal" child. The adolescent argues that clothing change does not necessarily mean a complete value change. He or she simply wants a chance to re-organize and re-define the order of values. The adolescents want to "decide for themselves."

Punk dress and image started more than fifteen years ago among a group of lower class British youth with no hope to move up in a rigid class society. They developed a hopeless nihilism which was expressed by their extreme clothing and hair styles. The punk look was adopted in the U.S.A. by predominantly middle class teens who sought to express their uniquess through these "street" fads turned fashion. The fashion became a connecting link between the heavy-metal, rock music as a visible symbol of the nihilistic themes expressed in the lyrics. In its most expressive form punk clothing encompassed head to foot changes such as orange hair, white powdered face, safety-pin earrings, black-leather motorcycle jackets studded with chrome gromets, tight jeans or short black leather skirts and round-toed black shoes. Entrepreneurs were able to turn the fad into profits from street-vendor sales to entire stores catering to the look. The punk phenomenon continues today. Some teens still cling to the complete look and lifestyle while others retain only the black clothing popularized by them. Adults are attracted to the short, black, leather and chrome garnished jackets and skirts first worn by these innovative adolescents. Punk clothing is truly the story of a "fad" that turned to "fashion.

Works Cited

Chilar, Kimberly. "The Many Sides of Sprouse," *Daily News Record* 12 Aug. 1988: 12.

Conklin, Ellis E. "Punk and Heavy Metal: Teen Rebellion or Something Darker!" *United Press International* 28 May 1985: np.

The Day My Kid Went Punk. Prod. Fern Field. ABC TV Special. Oct. 1987.

Gross, Michael. "Sprouse: Back in Fashion," *The New York Times* 9 June 1987: B. 6.

Hirshey, Gerri. "Styling for Dollars," *Washington Post Magazine* 21 Sept. 1986: 38.

Laws, Lynda. "Other Views: Mom Survives Spiked Hair, Studded Leather," *Los Angeles Times* 26 Aug. 1985, San Diego County Edition: View 5,1.

Leven, Pamela S. "They Keep It All in the Family," *American Banker* 20 Aug. 1987: 31.

Lewis, Fandy. "Pop Beat; Ready-Made Punk Attire Finds Commercial Niche," *Los Angeles Times* Orange County Edition, 7 June 1985: Calendar 6, 15.

Mason, John S. "Other Views: Silver Linings of a Parent's Nightmare," *Los Angeles Times* 27 Jan. 1986, View 5, 1.

Sager, Mike. "The Scene: It Looks Like Showing Off, But Punk Life is a Mean Hustle," *The Washingtonian.* April 1987: 181-88.

Sid and Nancy. 1986 Video.

Sones, Melissa. "British Designer, Vivienne Westwood; Vivienne Westwood and the Punk Legacy," *United Press International.* 11 Feb. 1986.

"When Punk Begins Sounding Passe, Das Furlines and Other Rockers Prove They're not too Proud to Polka," *People Magazine*. 9 Nov. 1987: 69.

Paper Clothes:
Not Just a Fad

Alexandra Palmer

"What's new in the paper today?"
"Well, my wife for one thing."
Ace Goodman, 1967

Paper clothes and household products were a shortlived but widespread phenomena from 1966-1968. Hundreds of thousands of paper garments were produced in North America yet, owing to their disposable and ephemeral nature, few of these survive.

The basis of western dress, whether considered a fashion or a fad, is newness and change. However, a brief but prevalent style, a fad, is often dismissed by historians as insignificant. Such occurrences may in fact be an amplification of a popular taste that should be seriously considered. The paper 'fad' of the middle 1960s, I suggest, is such an instance. Paper fashions perfectly represent the ideology and philosophy of the post-war generation who desired affordable, fashionable and futuristic design.

Fashion in the Sixties created a revolution in style and marketing. The achievements of the ready-to-wear and manufacturing industry prompted couturiers to license their names and open boutiques aimed at a young market with an average income. Paper garments were conceived and marketed for mass consumption. They appealed to the general public, both aesthetically and financially. As a manifestation of popular culture, the paper fashions of the 1960s provide an opportunity for a case study.

An investigation of the evolution of paper clothes in the Sixties, will demonstrate that paper dresses were a representative fashion in harmony with contemporary design trends and lifestyle. This will be achieved through an examination of the development and merchandising of paper garments, a look at the variety of events where they were worn and by the relationship made between paper fashions and contemporary art.

The first paper dresses were manufactured by the Scott Paper Company in late March 1966 (fig. 1 & 2. ROM #966.173.1 & 3). The motivation for making the dresses was to promote a new line of paper

85

Fig. 1 (ROM #966.175.1. Gift of Scott Paper Limited.)
Paper paisley dress. Manufactured by Scott Paper Co. 1966.

Fig. 2 (ROM #966.175.3. Gift of Scott Paper Limited)
Paper op art dress. Manufactured by Scott Paper Co. 1966.

napkins, toilet paper and paper towels called "Colorful Explosions" (Taylor "Fashions to Buy" 41; "Paper Capers" 71). With a coupon available from the table products, $1.00 and 25¢ postage, anyone could purchase, by mail-order, a fashionably styled and printed paper dress. Two models were made, and labeled "Paper Caper." They were produced in four sizes, one style, and two prints. One print was a black on white op-art design, the other of red, yellow and black with small paisleys. The A-line dresses were designed as sleeveless shifts with self-trimmed round necks and cut in two pattern pieces, with a hip patch pocket applied. By August, the Scott Paper Company had filled 500,000 orders, many of which were reorders from coupons packaged with the dress (Taylor "Fashions to Buy"). The staggering success achieved by the tremendous public interest and response to this venture was a surprise to the Scott Paper Company which had no long-term interest in the fashion market.

However, the potential of this market was picked up by other manufacturers. Mars Manufacturing Company of Asheville, N.C., producer of hosiery and swimsuits, in June 1966 were the first to break into the paper clothes market. Their paper fabric was printed by a gift-wrap company ("Throwaway Clothes" 6). Mars sold numerous prints and styles including op- art, paisley, paint-your-own-dress, bellbottom jumpsuits, men's vests and a silver foil shift made from a fabric used for insulating space suits (Taylor "Fashions to Buy" 41). By August Mars had shipped 120,000 of its original $1.29 dresses to department stores, and by 1967 the company had sold lines to J. C. Penney and Sears, Roebuck & Co. (Barmash "Public Tries" 10). Mars also developed disposable swimming trunks of Tyvek, a du Pont plastic, shipping 3,000 dozen, which were sold chiefly to hotels and motels, who made them available to guests poolside (Taylor "Fashions to Buy" 41).

In October of 1966 Moda-Mia, a division of Rayette-Faberge, Inc., launched their line of paper products. The line included sleeved and sleeveless shifts in Mexican prints for $2.00, with evening dresses, coats, blouses, and pants planned. These were packaged with instructions on how to cut them down if the buyer wished to create a new style. The garments were sold in supermarkets, drugstores and variety stores ("Paper clothes" 74).

Amelia Bassin, vice president for Moda-Mia, explained the appeal of paper clothes by comparing them to "...Saint Laurent's pop art dresses, for instance you could have the fun without spending the money" (Taylor "Fashions to Buy" 41). Saint Laurent, in fact, had borrowed Pop art images that had originally been taken from American popular culture. Paper dresses were really more closely related to American mass culture than to French couture models. The design sources available from street fashion for high fashion began to be acknowledged in the

Sixties. Saint Laurent recognized this and took advantage of it. His adoption of Pop imagery can be compared with his successful re-styling of the traditional pea jacket, and leather mod fashions into luxury models. Marylin Bender commented on this dissemination of ideas: "It (fashion in the 1960s) ceased to filter down from the top—from the haute couturiers and the women of educated taste whom they dressed—to the masses. It ascended from the populace to the plutocrat" (p.25).

Quickly paper fashions were made available, not only from manufacturers, but in boutiques and department stores, all of which responded to the public's favorable reaction to the garments. In Los Angeles Judith Brewer sold designer paper dresses in her boutique on Wiltshire Boulevard, which opened in July of 1966. She painted, or die-cut holes in dresses scalloping the hem and sleeves, or making an eyelet pattern. She designed a paper tennis dress, and a sleeveless, four tier flounced baby doll dress. The average retail price of her clothes was between ten and forty dollars. Custom paper jackets in neon-orange were made for The Beatles on their Los Angeles visit, and her 'fur coat' ($200.00), which was made of 100 yards of paper tied in bows, attracted wide-spread publicity ("Paper Clothes" 74; Carlton 134; Taylor "Fashion to Buy" 41). She also sold to I. Magnin's "News Stand" in-store paper boutique ("Real Live Paper Dolls" 52).

Elisa Daggs, of New York, soon became the most established 'paper couturier.' She opened her paper clothing business in the summer of 1966 ("Paper clothes" 74). Her first design was paper baby pinafores selling for five dollars a dozen at Neiman-Marcus. Soon after this success she was retailing at over sixty department stores ("Real Live Paper Dolls" 52). Some of Daggs' most popular designs included striped caftans, a strapless, striped, wrap-style mini dress, and an A-line tent dress propped out with a paper petticoat ("Wastebasket Dress" 134). Hats were designed by Adolfo II and Emme to match some of Daggs' clothes (Taylor "Paper Expands") and she even produced a wedding dress priced at $15.00 ("Now It's the Little Paper Dress" 134).

In June of 1967 Caroline Little and William Guggenheim III opened a boutique named "In Dispensable Disposables," on East 60th Street in Manhattan. The business partners were both in their late twenties and were typical of a generation of entrepreneurs who served their contemporaries. The younger generation was creating and selling fashion and furnishings that were distinct from those of their parents and geared to their own generation (Whiteley 80). "In Dispensable Disposables" was dedicated to replaceable and disposable fashions, selling sunglasses, evening dresses, raincoats, hats, and transparent dresses printed with glow in the dark paint (Taylor "An East Side Boutique" 24). The paper fashion rage was well underway.

Paper for fashion was in such demand that in January of 1967 there was a shortage of paper for garments. Elisa Daggs said, "We couldn't fill spring orders. The stores lived through a period of horror. It's a miracle anyone survived" ("Now It's the Little Paper Dress" 132). Though Daggs' statement may appear to be melodramatic, it is a reflection of the frenzy and interest the paper products engendered in both the manufacturing and public sector. The crisis was compounded by a fear that the interest in paper clothing would suddenly wane overnight and it was imperative, from a manufacturing perspective, to be able to meet the demand while it lasted.

The 'paper' itself was not actually paper, in the trade it is called a 'non-woven.' Scott's dresses were made from their patented Dura-Weve, a non-woven tissue with cellulose (wood pulp) strengthened by a rayon mesh ("Now It's the Little Paper Dress" 134). The 'paper' fabrics were produced by a binding process similar to felting, an inexpensive process since no spun threads or weaving was involved ("Non-Wovens & 'Paper' " 68). The Scott Paper Company had developed this in 1958 for use in disposable protective clothing and linens for hospitals and laboratories ("Scott Answer" 60).

The speed with which the manufacturing and marketing of the dresses was accomplished testified to the advances of the American garment industry that managed to produce these clothes at 'disposable prices.' The profits from paper clothes attracted over sixty manufacturers, with sales estimated at between $50 million to $100 million in a year ("Now It's the Little Paper Dress" 132). Paper fabric wholesaled for 8¢— 10¢ a yard, and it was hoped it would soon become cheaper ("Paper clothes" 73). However, it was still necessary to fabricate a paper garment using the same production costs and techniques as the identical garment made in a cloth. It was the sheer volume of paper clothes and the inexpensive production of the fabric, that made it possible for paper clothes to be a money making venture. By the end of 1966 national sales of paper garments amounted to $3.5 million (Brockhouse 38), this was a small percentage of the $30 billion sold in women's wearing apparel. However, it was a significant amount for such a low-priced and novel item. In 1967, Sterling Company hoped to make $6 million from the sale of paper garments (Brockhouse 37).

Technology still had to catch up with the product if production costs were to be reduced. This was hoped to be solved with a heat sealant, that would eliminate sewing ("The Future"). A heat sealant was already developed for vinyl, but was not available for paper products until the early 1970s (Guerrier 60). Future schemes and hopes included textile designer, Julian Tomchin's, prediction that paper garments would eventually be sold in tear-off rolls, and sold for pennies (Carlton 137).

The public's interest in paper clothes produced more elaborate styles. Zippers, velcro and snap fastenings were added to garments and the cloth was treated as any woven and more durable fabric. In the spring of 1967 paper fabric was finally available to the home sewing market and ranged in price from Paperworks' handscreened at 25¢ a yard, Kaycel's at 50¢ a yard and Tiger Fabrics at 99¢ a yard (Zill 84; "Non-Wovens" 69). Anyone could make anything from paper fabric. *Consumer Bulletin* ("Paper Chase" 6) recommended several Butterick and McCall's patterns and advised cutting deep armholes to avoid tearing, while *Look* (Zill 81) suggested using Vogue Couturier patterns. One year after the first Scott paper dress the kinds of clothes made privately and commercially ranged from bridal dresses, pants suits, slippers and hats, to a man's suit. Dresses were made in numerous prints and colors, and could be purchased or made on a whim; it was affordable to be daring.

The ability to mass-produce paper dresses so quickly led to escalating complexity in paper dress construction, ignoring the logic of a simple assembly for a garment with such a short life-span. This is revealed by an examination of an Elisa Daggs paper evening dress that sold for $6.00 (M.M.A., Costume Institute #1986.91.6). The dress is floor length and silk screened with wide stripes in orange, purple, yellow and pink. It is composed of eight pattern pieces; one front/back piece, a side/front/back, two back gores, two shoulder straps and a pair of ties. It has a self-faced bib front cut in one and folded with the vertically striped front. A seam joins a pink to an orange stripe at left side front. The dress wraps around in an A-line to center back. Two pink gores are matched and added at the center back hem completing the flare. Ties and shoulder straps are added and top-stitched. The pattern layout of this paper dress is developed as it would be for a cloth dress, with care taken to match the stripes at the seams. Little use is made of the paper quality of the material that has no grain, and little care for its transience.

Such sartorial excess for paper garments led Harry Gordon, a graphic artist, to rebel. He wanted to promote the paper quality of the garments and treat them as a canvas. His "Poster Dresses" sold for $3.00 and offered a choice of five motifs. They were all the same cut; a sleeveless, A-line shift, with only shoulder and side seams. The dresses were decorated with large photographic blow-ups covering the entire surface of the front. The images were of a cat, a rose, an eye, a rocket taking off which was enlarged from a news photograph, and a hand with the palm open in the Buddhist peace sign gesture, and printed with a first edition Allen Ginsberg poem ("Put-on Posters" 10). All were popular images and once worn took on the form of a wearable poster, affirming McLuhan's theories in the contemporary bestseller, *The Medium is the Massage* (1967).

Paper fabric was only one facet of a societal obsession with novelty and modern technology which was causing rapid changes in all aspects of daily life. Other man-made fabrics also took on a new look. *Life Magazine* ("Non-Seamstresses" 67-68) featured a double page spread of Lauren Hutton modeling Betsey Johnson's glue-it-yourself vinyl dress. This was a $15.00 transparent mini shift that could be purchased with a choice of kits. Each $5.00 kit contained adhesive-backed colorful foil scallops. The replacement and choice of scallops applied allowed the purchaser to create an individual design from a pre-assembled and packaged garment, the same way one could cut away areas of a paper dress. The wearer was encouraged to display their individuality and creativity through custom cutting or sticking, however little skill and time were required. The same type of pre-packaged flexibility appeared in an Emmanuelle Khanh of Paris dress made from strips of colored leather held together horizontally around the body with metal snap fastenings. It too was conceived with easy to redesign options. The snaps allowed the wearer to lower or shorten the length, by removing a strip, or to separate it into a skirt and top. Both dresses were available at the boutique "Paraphernalia" which specialized in the latest mod fashions.

Andy Warhol described the shop aptly:"...almost everything in the store would disintegrate within a couple of weeks, so that was really Pop...Paraphernalia had become a really mass boutique, which was sort of a contradiction—now if you designed for them, you had to be able to make LOTS of whatever you made, enough to send out to their stores all over the country. The masses wanted to look non-conformist, so that meant the nonconformity had to be mass-manufactured" (1983, 178). This is what the individualizing of the stick-and-cut approach to fashion achieved.

Similarly, paper dresses were available in numerous styles and prints, all of which could be customized with a pair of scissors and all intended to have a very limited life span, thereby guaranteeing that the wearer could not become old fashioned. They were a truly democratic fashion that was affordable by everyone who chose to wear the most recent style and material. The assertions, "In mass culture, it ain't what you do but the way you do it" and "Social acceptance can be won with a wardrobe" (Bender 18) can be admirably applied to paper garments.

The imaginative products made of paper related materials was endless. Baby cribs, tables, beach chairs, four lunch boxes in a picnic hamper that unfolded to make a tablecloth, a collapsible sun lounge, beach towels, curtains, bedspreads, hats, and slippers ("New this Year" 104-111). One entrepreneur made paper raincoats for dogs, with matching dresses and coats for the mistress. Cast-a-Ways of New York, was developing a "Fix-a-Flat" kit consisting of paper overalls and gloves

(Brockhouse 39). Such products indicate the aspirations of a society seeking objects with which to create a portable lifestyle that could be discarded and replaced at convenience. Stores such as "In Dispensable Disposables" and "Paperworks" in New York, sold paper furnishings and clothes catered specifically to this public demand.

The post-war generation's rebellion against the status quo was represented by these ephemeral objects which also attempted to satiate the desire for the most contemporary. Durability was not important as it was assumed that one would have money at hand to replace an object, and that the replacement would be more modern and therefore more pleasing.

This search for a disposable lifestyle was also reflected in a more casual attitude towards sex. Sexual encounters no longer necessarily meant marriage and a permanent relationship. Paper dresses were an indication of this social change and embodied a liberated attitude. To appear in public in a short, sleeveless, slip-like garment was the fashion; to wear this in paper connoted an avant-garde posture that did not fear its ripping and the subsequent possibility of bodily exposure, from what little was still left covered. Paper clothes were far more forward and therefore better than an ordinary mini dress.

The underlying sexual tension evoked by the wearing of paper dresses is borne out by Marion Lynch who when she first wore a paper dress to a party received too much male attention for comfort and said "...as the evening wore on, the dress wore out" (Newman). She was not inclined to repeat the experience. The popular press of the time frequently alluded to the risks of wearing paper clothing. Much humour was spent on the fact that the most destructive element was liquid on the fabric and this was most likely to occur at cocktail parties where the dresses were often worn. Elisa Daggs summed it up, "If you spill, you're dead" ("Wastebasket Dress" 134).

In reality the dresses were quite tough. A wear-test was conducted by a woman who wore the dress every day for a month while doing housework ("Wastebasket Dress" 136). It was the anticipatory nature of the garment that actually unsettled a wearer such as Ms. Lynch. One assumes, historically, that once a garment is sewn and made-up that it is relatively tough and will incur damage only due to great misfortune and maltreatment. The armorial nature of paper clothes was frail in comparison to cloth, thereby heightening the excitement of wearing such a garment. No doubt paper created a high level of apprehension, for a possible social disaster was an inherent hazard.

However, a more real concern was the potential fire risk in wearing paper. A Federal Trade Commission report concluded that the paper cloth met the standards of the Flammable Fabrics Act ("F.T.C."). The fabrics were treated with a fire retardant which was, in fact, the primary reason why the clothes could not be washed. Both wet and dry-cleaning removed the fire-retardant chemicals. This posed no problem since the major selling feature of the garments was their disposable nature, which negated the need and drudgery of cleaning ("Paper Chase" 4). Paper fabric designer Julian Tomchin said, "It's right for our age. After all who is going to do laundry in space?" ("Wastebasket Dress" 137).

The original success of Scott's publicity and promotional campaign was perpetuated in an assortment of public and private events. One of the first important social occasions styled around paper dress fashions was the Paper Dress Ball, held October 23, 1966 at the Wadsworth Atheneum, Connecticut. It was a benefit for the museum's building fund. Seven hundred guests came, many in 'designer' paper dresses commissioned especially for the event. Tziam Lukus, a fabric designer, was requested by the museum to design six paper dresses, all of which were later donated. One was floor length and printed in red, white and blue to compliment Mrs. Rebekah Harkness' Salvador Dali brooch worn on the occasion. Rudi Gernreich made a transparent plastic dress with circular colored paper decals placed in a few discrete spots. This was modeled at midnight by Peggy Moffitt of the topless bathing suit fame. "I guess you might call it peep art" Gernreich commented (Klemesrud "But Will" 45). It was the creation of such events that prompted Marilyn Bender to write about paper dresses:

No need to worry that such a democratic dress—one that absolutely anyone can afford— will destroy the fashion elite. The woman of wealth and social contacts can commission an artist to create a special paper dress for a special event, then donate it to a museum, provided the garment hasn't deteriorated on the dance floor. (16)

A similar event was held the following year in New York City aboard the ocean liner, Michelangelo. It was a fund raising dinner for the Police Athletic League. Again, rich socialites commissioned custom paper dresses. Bill Blass took the disposable concept to the extreme with an evening dress of cheetah print on brown paper. He trimmed the long sleeves with sable cuffs; a metaphor for the size of the disposable income available for such lavish, disposable clothes. For Miss Wendy Vanderbilt, Sarmi made a pink paper mini dress with a ruffled hem that dipped to the floor in the back. Although this is a style traditionally associated with taffeta fabric, the paper dress was successful due to its stiff hand. The evening culminated in a "glamourous wear-a-while fashion show" held at midnight when fifteen of the attending socialites modeled their gowns under a spotlight (Klemesrud, "Michelangelo" 52; "High-Fashion" 123). This tradition was well established by such events as Junior League fashion shows but made more alluring by the position models had recently attained in the public eye.

Models in the Sixties were a new type of celebrity. Public notoriety was no longer necessarily conferred on the upper crust and movie stars; rather on the artists, writers, models, hairdressers and those who pushed conventional styles and standards forward. Andy Warhol describes this erosion of social classes and segregation, "It was fun to see the Museum of Modern Art people next to the teeny-boppers next to the amphetamine queens next to the fashion editors" (162). Paper garments contributed to this as status could no longer be easily ascertained through dress.

A girl could achieve fame and fortune by becoming a model. Books such as *How to be a Model* by Suzy Menkes, an English fashion editor, advertised a modeling competition sponsored by the publisher and *19 Magazine* (143-144). Jean Shrimpton wrote her autobiography and vied with Jacqueline Kennedy for media attention. The boundaries of a formally structured social hierarchy were eroding, with social success measured by the modernity of your appearance. "Fashion wasn't what you wore someplace anymore; it was the whole reason for going" (Warhol 87).

The extensive interest generated by paper garments is exhibited by the diversity of places where the clothes were worn, and by the spectrum in age and social position of those who wore them. A benefit in Washington had the guests trade in their Dior clothes to be auctioned, and in return were given paper dresses to wear. Mrs. Kennedy was one of the guests (Chamberlin 33). The Duchess of Windsor, who was on the 'Best Dressed List' wore a paper dress thus providing a role model for older and more conventional women to wear them. Two housewives living in New England opened their own shop, "Paper Doll" (Karpen 58). In France a concert pianist wore a paper jacket made by Pierre Cardin and cut off the sleeves before the performance, the American artist Robert Rausenberg, had a suit tailored from grocery-bag paper (Chamberlin 33).

A party was usually associated with the wearing of paper dresses. Hallmark produced a line of complete party accessories with a matching dress that was available on a mass scale in drugstores (Chamberlin 33). A hostess could co-ordinate her personal appearance with the plates, napkins, table cloth, coasters, place cards, and gift wrappings thus associating herself directly with the center of the entertainment. The selling of paper dresses in drugstores and supermarkets underscored the convenience of purchasing new clothes. A party, including party clothes, could be put together on the spur of the moment.

In this same vein Whippette Sportswear Co., invented "Le Canned Dress" (Fig. 3. ROM # 966.280). It was made of nylon and came in three styles, a choice of colors, sizes 5-13, and cost $25.00 (Nemy 34). It was sold in a tin can with a brightly colored label. Though it was retailed in department stores, the marketing of it in a can fostered the

Fig. 3. (ROM #966.280a-d. Gift of Louben Sportswear Inc.)
Le Canned Dress, 1966. Manufactured by Whippette Sportswear Co.

idea that the dress was as available as a tin of soup in a supermarket, promoting the ideology of affordable, fashionable clothing for everyone.

Private 'paper parties,' encouraged by such companies as Hallmark, were numerous. Not to be outdone by these, Mrs. Leon Meltzer of Philadelphia held a dinner dance and sent all her one hundred female guest the same floor length green, white and black paisley paper dress in which to attend the function. She was "...intrigued with the idea of a party where all the women were dressed alike" (Newman 1). The irony was that she made the nonconformity and modernity of the paper dresses a uniform and a social obligation, thereby negating the daring image, and challenging her guests not to conform by wearing normal cloth evening clothes.

The business and advertising world took great advantage of the interest in paper clothes. Air India held a 'happening' in New York City at the Lotos Club, to unveil a paper sari (Fig. 4). Three models were hired to demonstrate the wearing of the garment and mingle with the guests ("Paper at the Lotos" 30). The saris were six yards long and were available from Air India for $5.00 by mail-order with a booklet "on how to put the thing on" (Chamberlin 36). The press release announced it as "a mod, mod PAPER SARI" that was designed by Elisa Daggs. The event and the sari combined a number of contemporary trends; a party, models modeling and providing a hostess function, a paper garment that went beyond a mini dress, and that was designed by the most famous paper fashion designer.

TIME Magazine also was swift to adopt the attention getting paper dresses for their own promotion. A sleeveless white paper dress was made and printed in black with 'TIME,' in op-art graphics. It was trimmed with black cotton piping at the neck and armscye, and made in two sizes, "too big" and "too small" (Fig. 5. ROM # 967.77). The designers were Walter Lefmann and Ron de Vito in TIME's Promotion department. The dresses were placed in a red rectangular box, with a card reading: "For Your ValenTIME....For every week in homes like yours across the country, some six million women slip into a little black-and-white print that just fits their taste and interests: TIME, The Weekly Newsmagazine." This packet was sent to all clients on the consumer promotion list. TIME's internal newsletter, *FYI*, of 10th February 1967, included a photograph of the female staff in the Business and Promotions departments all wearing the dress. In Ottawa a paper fashion show was held by TIME and the Travel Industry Association of Canada to promote resort vacationing and disposable paper resort clothes in which the TIME dress was featured (Earl).

Abraham & Strauss, in Brooklyn, was one of the first department stores to open a division of Mars Manufacturing Co., 'The Waste Paper Boutique,' in September 1966. In November Abraham & Strauss invited

Fig. 4. (Photography by Anthony Hyde, Jr. courtesy of Air India)
Air India paper sari, designed by Elisa Daggs, 1967.

Fig. 5. (ROM #967.77. Gift of Time International of Canada Ltd.)
TIME paper dress, 1967.

Andy Warhol to promote a Mars Co. paper dress sold with a paint kit. The paint kit and performance by Warhol helped to instill the idea of fashion as a creative and artistic pursuit. The dress was made in two pieces, the same cut front and back, with a shaped raglan short sleeve. It was piped at the neck and cuff with red and white striped cotton. The watercolour paint kit had six colors and a brush (M.M.A. Costume Institute # 1986.91.7ab). Nico, the singer with the Velvet Underground, wore the dresses of "whitest white twill of Kaycel R" (Warhol 191) while Warhol painted them. On one he silkscreened "FRAGILE" down the front in bright magenta while she was lying on a table, and signed it 'Dali' (Brooklyn Museum #66.237.1). On another he glued large silkscreened paper bananas, two in front and two behind (Brooklyn Museum #66.237.2). Both dresses were donated to the Brooklyn Museum validating the event as an art happening and the dresses as art objects ("Painting on the Dress" 49).

Paper dresses united art, fashion and entertainment, all of which were increasingly becoming part of the developing popular culture. The integration of contemporary art into daily life by the populace really came about in the Sixties. Pop art had been taken up by the art, advertising, fashion and design worlds. Public awareness of an artist such as Andy Warhol, who could be used as a marketing tool for paper dresses, was a new occurrence and possible by the growth of information and media technology. Already Pop fashions, such as a sleeveless shift printed with a large Campbell's soup tin, had been manufactured and sold (Constable 62). Art was sold as a fashion style, with the actual design of the garment acting as a support for the image.

The choice of an op-art print for the first Scott dresses was in perfect harmony with the times. The "Responsive Eye" Op-Art exhibition held at the Museum of Modern Art in 1965 promoted the latest movement in the art world. Op-Art was immediately transferred into fabric and household designs. Tzaium Lukus was one of the most successful and noted op-art fabric, and later dress, designers. Larry Aldrich commissioned fabric designer Julian Tomchin to adapt Bridget Riley paintings into textiles ("It's Op" 53). *American Fabrics* was swift to take up the call of op-art for fabric design calling it "...a healthy departure from the meretriciousness and superficial existentialism of Pop art..." ("Op-Art in Textile" 83), and was as quick to denounce Pop art as passe, having just lauded it in the previous issue as a "...sophisticated, witty meeting between popular culture and high art" ("Art and Textiles" 79). This quick about face and anxiousness to keep up with the very latest developments in art and fashion, and the need to not appear old fashioned, even by a few months or weeks, was the type of climate receptive to the modern styled and printed disposable clothing. In fact *American*

Fabrics' attention to the youth culture and art scene was perceived as requisite in order to understand and anticipate public demand for fashion.

Op-Art lent itself very well to fabric design. The illusion of movement based upon the eye's optic nerve, hence the name, could only be furthered by application to fabric and an object which actually moved and made the optical, hallucinatory effects even more pronounced and disorienting. Anne Werher reminisced about this, "I went through an extended op-art phase, always black and white and dizzy-busy. I deliberately wore these costumes to op-art shows" (Melinkoff 151). It became increasingly difficult to differentiate between what was the art. Was it the dress or was it a canvas, or the person who wore the canvas?

Clean lines, geometric shapes and the use of stiff fabrics initiated by Courreges with his famous 1964 Space Age Collection, made the non-draping quality of paper fabrics, vinyl, chains and plastics an asset to design, as clear silhouettes were easily achieved. The demand for these garments was based upon the utilization of new materials and a celebration of modern technology. These clothes put into immediate use the very latest materials for a large youthful public who wanted to wear, sit on and live with the latest thing, at least for as long as it was the very latest.

This futuristic thinking was epitomized by the success of Tiger Morse, a New York fashion designer, who was "dedicated to the future and to the materials of the future, plastic, synthetics, glass, paper, found objects and anything else that may come along" ("Tiger Morse" 89). Tiger opened a small boutique called "Teeny-Weeny" at Madison and 73rd Streets (Bender 66). Similarly, Paco Rabanne had successfully launched his metal dresses ("Pieced in Plastic" 53) and by 1967 the latest technological dress was vinyl and lit up. It was designed by Diana Dew and sold at Paraphernalia ("Turn On" 80).

Two exhibitions at the Museum of Contemporary Crafts, New York, in 1967 and 1968, "Made with Paper" and "Body Covering," helped to expand the growing interest in space age technology, and the possibilities of paper. "Body Covering" (15 April-9 June 1968) dealt with a large variety of materials, from tattooing to the latest space travel equipment and Diana Dew's "Movie dress" made from leather inset with illuminated photographs and operated by a power pack (*Body Covering* 37).

"Made with Paper" (18 November-7 January 1968) was designed with modular sections of reinforced paper screens as the installation material. The artifacts covered a wide range of objects from chairs, lights, and flooring materials to clothes. The public was encouraged to wear paper slippers which were provided at the exhibit entrance. Among the paper clothes displayed were hats, dresses, a man's shirt, and a tufted paper coat by Bonnie Cashin as well as her paper hats. Cashin's interest in paper stemmed from the early 1950s when she made herself some bright colored paper tote bags. In 1968 she formed a corporation called "Bonnie Cashin's Paper-Route to Fashion" ("Bonnie Cashin's" 129).

The declining demand for paper clothes, from 1968 onwards, was not a failure of the designs or the fabrics, but a reflection of the general shift in design trends and social philosophy. Mod and Pop style was supplanted by the 'back-to-nature' hippie lifestyle. Ecological issues were fought against pollution and waste, often the same waste that was just produced.

In 1971 the Disposables Association held a three-day seminar and exhibit. One of the concerns and recommendations was to change the name of the organization since "... the word 'disposable' itself can be a red flag to the youth culture, because of the widespread concern with the problem of solid wastes" (Guerrier 59). What had been an asset to sales and what had been associated with convenience and modernism was already a few years later considered in a contrary light.

The lasting business for disposables has been in hospitals and other areas where disposable clothing and cloth is more cost effective than laundry charges ("Now It's the Little" 133). This was the market Scott originally pursued with paper fabric before its paper dress publicity campaign. Today we give little thought to wearing and throwing away 'contaminated' paper garments in nuclear plants, hospitals, or at home with baby's diapers. The convenience and economical aspect of paper clothes has replaced the fun and hope-filled futuristic designs of the middle Sixties.

Paper garments achieved the most desirable components of mid-Sixties design. They combined the most contemporary art forms in the print and colors, style with a unique garment was an easy matter to adjust with a pair of scissors. The cost was so marginal that anyone could afford the image. If you were willing to be a 'swinger' paper clothes could be bought in a department store, boutique, or around the corner in the supermarket or drugstore. If you were not sure about your purchase and lost the confidence to wear it, the product was easily disposable, and the monetary guilt often associated with extravagance need not apply. If you did wear the dress, the novelty of the object and the wearing of it would only last for an evening or two, and future developments in styles and materials could be immediately pursued. Little investment in shopping time or money were involved.

The short-lived public interest in paper clothes was in stride with other contemporary design and social trends that sought similar quick and disposable answers to daily life. Fashion provided an experimental forum for the newest styles and materials, one of which was paper, that were financially and aesthetically successful within the framework of the time. Paper clothes should be considered in this context as a clear expression of popular culture. "In the Sixties, fashion stopped being clothes and became a value, a tool, a way of life, a kind of symbolism" (Bender 43).

Works Cited

"Aglow." *New Yorker* 28 Jan. 1967: 26-8.

"All dressed up in paper." *Chemical Week* 2 Mar. 1986: 18.

Ames, Elinor. "Paper Wedding Dress." *Daily News* 16 Feb. 1967: 52.

"Art and Textiles—From Primitive to Pop." *American Fabrics* Winter 1964-65: 76-83.

Barmash, Isadore. "Public Tries on Paper-Clothing Fad for Size." *New York Times* 22 Jan. 1967: III.1+.

Bender, Marylin. *The Beautiful People.* New York: Coward-McCann, Inc., 1967.

" 'Bonnie Cashin's Paper-Route to Fashion.' " *American Fabrics* Spring 1968: 129.

Brockhouse, Robert A. "How Paper is Invading the Textile Market." *Paper Trade Journal* 25 Sept. 1967: 36-40.

———. "But Don't Go Near the Water." *Sales Management* 1 Apr. 1967: 58+.

Carlton, Helen. "The Wastebasket Dress Has Arrived." *Life* Nov. 1966: 132-37.

"Chain Reaction." *Time* 7 June 1968: 60.

Chamberlin, Anne. "The Paper Caper." *Saturday Evening Post* 2 Dec. 1967: 33-7.

"Clothes that Glisten: the Economical Way to 'Party Time'." *Consumer Bulletin* Nov. 1967: 35.

Constable, R. "Styles Too are Pushed Further by Pop." *Life* 26 Feb. 1965: 59-60+.

"Dress for Non-seamstresses." *Life* 29 July 1966: 68-70.

Earl, Larry. Telephone interview. 14 Jan. 1988.

"F.T.C. Study Made of Paper Dresses." *New York Times* 26 Jan. 1967: 44.

"The Future—Get With It!" *American Fabrics* Fall 1968: 62.

Goodman, Ace "All the Nudes that Fit the Print." *Saturday Review.* 22 July 1967: 6.

Greenberg, Pearl. "Haute Couture in Paper Dresses." *School Arts* Feb. 1969: 29-30.

Guerrier, James J. "Disposables: Self-appraisal in Retrospect at IDEA 71." *Pulp & Paper* Feb. 1972: 59-61.

"High-Fashion Paper Ball with Reemay Fashions Held on S.S. Michelangelo To Benefit PAL." *American Fabrics* Fall-Winter 1967: 123.

Hyman, Tom. "Turn on Your Dress Diana!" *Saturday Evening Post* 13 Jan. 1968: 26-9.

"An Institute Report on Paper Clothing." *Good Housekeeping* 6 Aug. 1967: 6.

"It's Op from Top to Toe." *Life* 16 Apr. 1965: 52-4.

Karpen, Marian. "The Paper Explosion." *Women's Wear Daily* 31 May 1967: 58.

Klemesrud, Judy. "But Will Paper Dresses Pass the Test of Time?" *New York Times* 24 Oct. 1966: 45.

———. "Aboard the Michelangelo, Gowns Were Paper but Chic." *New York Times* 16 Nov. 1967: 52.

Levy, R. "Wardrobes for the Wastebasket." *Duns Review* June 1967: 59.

Made with Paper. New York: Museum of Contemporary Crafts, 1967.

McLuhan, Marshall. *The Medium is the Massage.* New York: Bantam Books, Inc., 1967.

McSweeney, Edward. "Which Way Will the Paper Tiger Jump?" *Pulp & Paper* 5 Dec. 1966: 38-40.

Melinkoff, Ellen. *What We Wore.* New York: Quill, 1984.

Menkes, Suzy. *How to be a Model.* London: Sphere Books, Ltd., 1969.

Morris, Bernadine. "Paper Dresses Ideal for Little Cutups." *New York Times* 7 Jan. 1967: 16.

Nemy, Enid. "If Laughter Could Be Canned So Could Fashion, He Thought." *New York Times* 9 Nov. 1966: 34.

"New This Year—Summer's Dashing Toss-Aways." *House & Garden* June 1967: 104-11.

Newman, Clarence. "Wrap Her in Paper: Cheap, New Frocks Are Hit With Women." *Wall Street Journal* 4 Oct. 1966: 1.

"Non-Wovens & 'Paper'—The Web Textiles." *American Fabrics* Summer 1967: 68-9.

"Now! Here! Soon! Paper Money Will Buy Paper Suits." *Advertising Age* 22 February 1966: 16.

"Now It's the Little Paper Dress." *Business Week* 22 July 1967: 132-34+.

"Op Art in the Fabric-Fashion Market." *American Fabrics* Spring 1965: 35

"Op Art in Textile Print Design." *American Fabrics* Spring 1965: 81-7.

"Paint in It. Play in It. Its Paper, so Have a Good Time in It." *Vogue* Oct. 1966: 262.

"The Painting on the Dress Said 'Fragile'." *New York Times* 11 No. 1966: 49.

"Paper at the Lotos." *New Yorker* 27 May 1967: 29-30.

"Paper clothes: a Wardrobe to Throw Away." *Business Week* July 1966: 73-4.

"Paper Capers." *Time* 18 March 1966: 71.

"Paper Chase—the Throw-away Fashion. The Boom in Disposable Clothes." *Consumer Bulletin* July 1967: 4-6.

"Paper Dresses Show Increase In Sales." *New York Times* 4 Dec. 1966: F15.

"Paper Fashions." *Seventeen* May 1967: 142-45.

"Papered Over." *Newsweek* 31 Oct. 1967: 105.

"Paper Yarn Catching On." *Business Week* 26 Feb. 1963: 66+.

Pehowski, Marian. "Throw-Away Clothes." *Science News Letter* 19 May 1956: 314-15.

"Pieced in Plastic." *Time* 8 Apr. 1966: 53.

"Pioneering In Paper Clothing." *Nations Business* Oct. 1980: 68.

Pouch, N.L.. "It Really Is Paper!" *Good Housekeeping* 14 Aug. 1967: 144.

"Put On Posters." *Life* 5 Apr. 1968: 39-40.

Quant, Mary. *Quant by Quant*. London: Cassell & Co. Ltd., 1966.

"Real Live Paper Dolls." *Time* 17 Mar. 1966: 52.

"Scott Answer to Oversupply: Dura-Weve." *Pulp & Paper* Aug. 1958: 60.

Shorr, Mimi (ed.) *Body Covering*. New York: Museum of Contemporary Crafts, 1968.

Shrimpton, Jean. *The Truth About Modeling*. London: W. H. Allen, 1964.

Taylor, Angela. "Fashions to Buy, Wear and Then Throw Away." *New York Times* 19 Aug. 1966: 41.

———. "Paper Expands Its Domain: Wedding Dresses, Shoes & Bikinis." *New York Times* 6 Mar. 1967: 42.

———. "An East Side Boutique Dedicated to Disposability." *New York Times* 10 June 1967: 24.

"Throwaway Clothes on the March." *American Fabrics* Fall-Winter 1966: 6.

"Tiger Morse—Go-Go Extravaganza." *American Fabrics* Fall-Winter 1966: 88-91.

"Turn On: Turn Off." *Time* 20 Jan. 1967: 80.

"Wardrobes for the Wastebasket." *Duns Review* July 1967: 59.

Warhol, Andy. *POPism: The Warhol '60s.* (1980, New York: Harper & Row.) New York: Colophon ed., 1983.

"Wastebasket Dress Has Arrived." *Life* 25 Nov. 1966: 132-37.

Wharton, Don. "How Soon Will We Wear Paper Clothes?" *Reader's Digest* Aug. 1966: 53-5.

Whiteley, Nigel."Interior Design In the 1960s: Arenas for Performance." *Art History* 1 March 1987: 79-90.

Wilson, Elizabeth. *Adorned in Dreams: Fashion and Modernity*. London: Virago, 1985.

"You Couldn't Really Say They Have That Ye-Ye Look." *FYI* Internal Time newsletter. 10 Feb. 1967: 2.

Zill, Jo Ahern. "Paper Posh. Disposable Elegance." *Look* 7 March 1967: 80-4.

Abbreviations
ROM Royal Ontario Museum (Toronto)
MMA Metropolitan Museum of Art (New York City)

Senior Cords:
A Rite of Passage

Pamela J. Schlick
and
Kathleen L. Rowold

A cherished privilege 'for seniors only' is that of wearing beloved senior cords! These cords are an institution reserved only for those who have attained that most glorious position—SENIORS! The underclassmen may eye with envy this wierd (sic) mode of dressing, but it's another one of those 'senior privileges' that make being a senior 'just grand!' (*Silhouette*)

Introduction

The collective appearance of a group can be considered one aspect of its popular culture. The clothing worn by a group or sub-group of a culture often indicates group membership or group association. This has often been referred to as associational (Flugel 132), distinctive, class, or ritualistic dress. Within ritualistic dress, items of apparel are often worn to signify rites of passage and rites of intensification.

Today, many of the clothing rituals related to rites of passage have lost their magico-religious affiliation and have developed into popular social celebrations. One such ritual is senior cords, the practice of high school and college seniors wearing personalized cream-colored corduroy skirts and trousers. Although originally intended to ceremonialize one of life's changes (passage into the adult world), Senior Cords developed into a popular art form that reflected student life from 1912-1972.

Rites of Passage and Intensification

The rite of passage, a ritualized celebration of life changes such as birth, puberty, marriage, pregnancy, parenthood, occupational or social changes and death, serves to ensure passage from one condition or social state to the next (Rowold 17).

The movement of a man through his life time, from womb to tomb, is punctuated by a number of critical moments of transition which all societies ritualize and publicly mark with available observations to impress the significance of the individual and the group on living members of the community. (Warner 567)

Although a ritual is most frequently associated with magic and religion, it can refer to any culturally patterned activity that is taken seriously by the participant or participants (Roach and Eicher 15). A rite of passage separates the individual from the rest of the group, relieves the individual's confusion and emotional stress of being separated from the old status, and publicly declares the individual's entry into the new status. Senior cords certainly functioned in this manner, for as one participant noted, "It [senior cords] was a good tradition that gave a feeling of security and pride" (Elliott).

Societies typically develop symbols that enable members affected by the transition to express their feelings in a clear manner. Much of the ceremony and symbolic behavior that accompanies a rite of passage involves dress and adornment (Rowold 19). This clothing is often new or special (Roach and Eicher 15) and can ease the transition from one role to another (Lurie 19).

The rite of intensification is a ritual which marks an occasion, crisis (Roach and Eicher 15) or event involving the community. It binds the community together at a crucial time to promote unity such as wearing a team's colors to a football game or pep rally (Kaiser 430). "I'll never forget the fun we had at football games in our painted senior cords!" (*Sargasso* 1957).

Senior cords suggest all of the characteristics of both a rite of passage and a rite of intensification. Expressive in every way, the aptly chosen cord-du-roi (cloth of kings) decoratively reflects the comical child as well as the emerging, nostalgic adult. "For the last time we wear our senior cords, proudly and sadly...now we are entering a new world" (*Sargasso* 1961).

Ours is a spirit of the young: optimism, joy, anticipation, and a touch of sadness. It is a sadness of realization. The realization that we can never return to the pleasant experiences of youth...never return to the carefree attitudes of youth. Each generation leaves these things as it matures. But the next generation adopts them and keeps them alive, carrying on where we left off until they, too, step into their places in the world. (*Aurora*)

Distinctive Dress

Of the various terms used to identify apparel worn to indicate group membership, distinctive dress is perhaps the most all-encompassing. Distinctive dress can be classified into two categories: 1) that which was created and worn in compliance with fixed, hierarchical (Flugel 132) criteria showing little or no variation and 2) that which was created and worn according to minimal criteria and often personalized for or by the wearer. Military, school, and occupational uniforms are examples of the first category. Variations usually occur only to indicate that the wearer has achieved a rite of passage by moving from one sub-group to the next (changing rank or school class).

...all the various kinds of 'fixed' costume that we have considered have a special (and often valuable) social significance, inasmuch as they indicate membership of a group, and are, in a way, symbolic of the feelings, sentiments, and interests that unite the groups; to wear them is a special privilege, which is jealously guarded, and the infringement of which is seldom attempted, or, if attempted, much resented. (Flugel 133)

Both the embroidered and embellished blue jeans worn in the 1960s by "hippies" which were symbolic of individual expression (Kaiser 439) and senior cords, which are symbolic of social identity, exemplify the second category. In some cases, a particular item of distinctive dress will bridge the two categories such as the recent practice of personalizing graduation mortar boards with messages.

The importance attached to particular features of dress that have become symbolic of special social privileges and respect can often be well seen in school life. In the absence of definite uniforms or other hierarchical costumes, items of...dress are apt to be treated as 'fixed' dress, to which only certain members of the community are entitled. (Flugel 133)

Class Dress In Indiana

Class dress, one type of distinctive dress, can be defined for our purposes as items of apparel or adornment worn only by members of a particular grade (or class) in high school or college. Class dress can include class rings, senior keys, sweaters, beanies or hats as well as senior cords. Research in this area is virtually untapped perhaps, because those involved assumed the wearing of these items was "a given"—"...almost everybody had them, just like a class ring it was a standard" (Elliott)— and thus left very little written documentation. Two sources, however, have been particularly useful for researching class dress in Indiana: personal reports in the form of oral history and survey data of persons who actually wore these items of dress, and archival research of high school and college yearbooks. Oral history and survey data collected for this research were solicited through news releases resulting in over 250 voluntary participants.

Archival records indicate that class dress may have first appeared in the State of Indiana at Indiana University in 1906. A calendar for that year shows that on "Nov. 8. Seniors decide to adopt the sombrero as the class hat" (see Figure 1) and on "Nov. 27. Juniors decide upon a golf jersey as class dress" (*Arbutus* 332). An account of the University's "Foundation Day" (see Figure 2) reports:

Fig. 1. Senior Sombreros. Photograph from 1906 *Arbutus* (259).

Fig. 2. Foundation Day Procession. Photograph from 1906 *Arbutus* (73).

Each class was resplendent with some distinctive feature. The Senior sombreros showed up bravely in line: the Juniors were noble and chesty in their efforts to present an impressive appearance with their old-gold jerseys just received; the Sophomores were decorated each with a red banner, hence-forth to be the color of the second year class; the Freshman magnanimously embraced in their ranks all persons not otherwise designated. (*Arbutus* 1906, 73-4)

In describing the golf jersey, the president of the junior class states,

It would be utterly impossible for a stranger visiting Indiana University and making the rounds of the campus not to be attracted by certain individuals, whom he would meet on every hand, who are classified on the college records as Juniors. They are conspicuous for two reasons: First, because of their impressive and prepossessing personalities; second, because of a peculiar and unique garb which they wear. The latter is really unnecessary. It is simply a safe-guard to prevent the slightest possibility of any one confusing them with the boorish and barbaric horde of Sophomores and Freshmen, especially the last named.

This garb is in the nature of a golf jersey, the color of which has been the subject of much discussion...However, if a Junior be consulted about the matter he will say that the shade is "old gold." (*Arbutus* 1906, 289)

It is unclear what influenced the adoption of the traditions of the senior sombrero and the junior golf jersey, nor is it known when these traditions ceased. One could surmise that the adoption of the sombrero versus another type of garment or style of hat is related to its similarity to the military campaign hat worn at the time. However, the disappearance of sombreros and golf jerseys did not mark the end of class dress.

Senior Cords

There are many symbols of senior superiority, but that of having senior cords is probably the one looked forward to most...(*Owl*)

The 1912 *Arbutus*, the Indiana University yearbook, shows a photograph of corduroy trousers encaptioned "Senior Pants—The Great Unwashed" (see Figure 3) but does not describe the tradition. Further, the 1913 *Arbutus* includes a poem entitled *Hail, Freshmen!* with the following excerpt:

And when, attired in Senior corduroys, THY time has come to strut as they do now— (78)

Senior cords were apparently well established at both Indiana and Purdue Universities by World War I, and had been accepted at DePauw University (McCoy) and some high schools by the late 1920s. Unlike senior sombreros and junior golf jerseys which were worn from their

Fig. 3. Senior Pants—The Great Unwashed. Photograph from 1912 *Arbutus* (12).

introduction by both men and women, the senior cord tradition began as a ritual for male students only (Eberhart). By the late 1920s, however, female students at some schools were wearing cord skirts (Wallace). Senior cords were always cream or camel-colored and styled according to the current fashion.

The susceptibility of high school studes [students] to fads has truly been noticible (sic) through-out the halls. Emphasis on draped trousers and 'frock' coats [zoot suits] was necessarily short-lived, but in their stead followed...highly decorative cords. (*Indian*)

Prior to 1920, cords at Indiana University were worn "blank", or were minimally decorated with phrases, club symbols and some autographs (Eberhart; see Figure 4). During the 1940s and 1950s, they were decorated extensively with classmates' autographs (Spangler; see Figure 5). Gradually, cords truly became an outlet for personal expression (see Figure 6). Symbols representing school clubs, sports mascots, favorite meeting places, cars, class rings, class plays and steady dates as well as television and movie caricatures were emblazoned on cords (see Figure 7). Cords were:"...walking scrapbooks" (Kirby), "...moving art galleries" (Classic Cords), "...a symbol of four years in high school" (Wichems), "...the very essence of high school" (Fox), and "...a chance to say out loud 'here's who I am' " (Young). Most cord decorations were two-dimensional, although there is some evidence of three-dimensional designs such as an occasional appliqued badge or mortarboard tassel. By the late 1950s, the location of specific symbols became important. The center front and center back of skirts and trousers were reserved for favorite activities or mottos and side seems were reserved for the name of the school and sports team (see Figure 8). "The decoration on the pants and skirts [was] limited only by the imagination of the wearer" (Harlan).

The late 1950s and early 1960s marked the height of cord popularity. "Getting our senior cords painted was just as important as getting our senior pictures taken" (Szwec). During this period, cords evolved into an art form, "My senior cords are a work of art!" (Hiam) Many students paid from $15 to $25 to have their cords decorated by an "expert," a fellow student or adult with artistic talent (see Figure 9). "Long consideration was given on how to decorate them, then great strides were taken to have every line perfectly drawn" (*Wigwam*). Students became fashion designers (Clensy). Cord artists were proud of their work. Even twenty years later, some cord artists could browse through a rack of Senior Cords and identify those they had painted.

The media used to decorate cords were related to both technology and aesthetic trends. Early cords were inscribed with India ink. Later, ball-point pens, felt-tip pens, and liquid embroidery were used. Colors

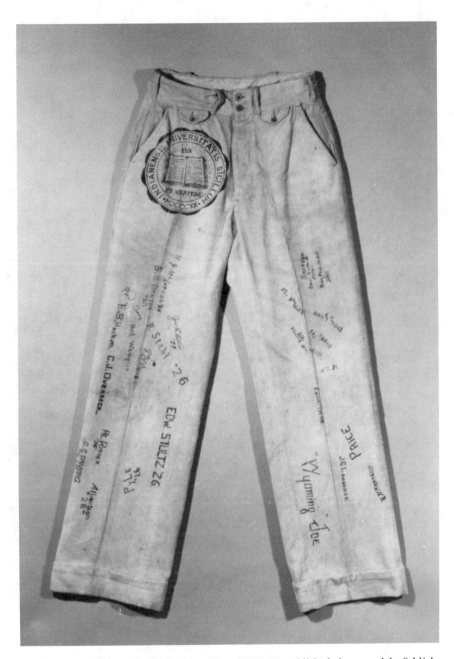

Fig. 4. Senior Cords: Indiana University, Class of 1926. Unpublished photograph by Schlick.

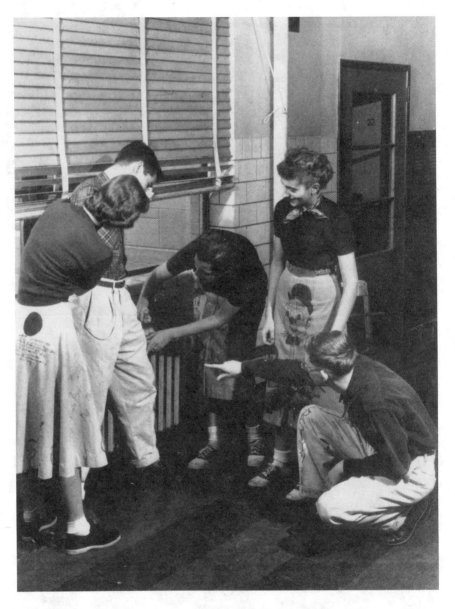

Fig. 5. Autographing Senior Cords. Photograph from 1952 *Jordannus* (31).

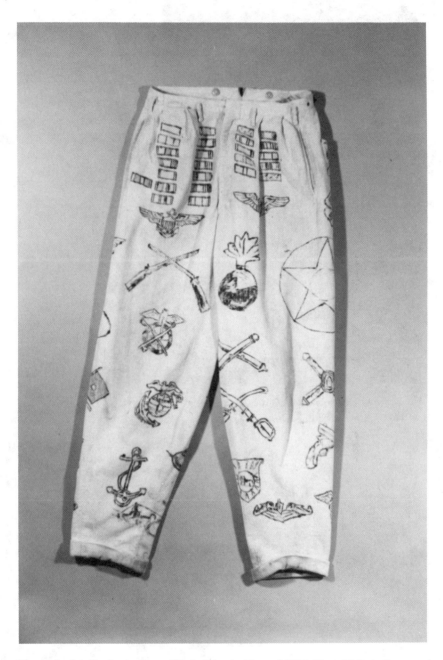

Fig. 6. Senior Cords: Anderson High School, Class of 1946. Unpublished photograph by Schlick.

Fig. 7. Senior Cords: Hartford City High School, Class of 1959. Unpublished photograph by Schlick

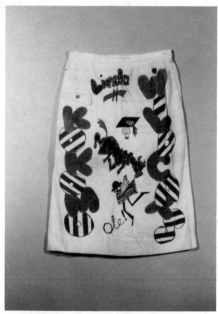

Fig. 8. Senior Cords: Kokomo High School, Class of 1963. Unpublished photograph by Schlick.

ranged from black or red in the 1920s to a multitude of bright colors by the 1970s.

Painted cords with colors bright
Around the halls made a dignified sight (*Sargasso* 1959)

Senior cords generally consisted of trousers or skirts. However, during the 1960s and 1970s, women wore shorts, vests, jumpers and jackets as well. "Blanks" or undecorated trousers were almost always purchased ready-to-wear, but many skirts, vests, and shorts were made at home.

Cords became such an integral part of Indiana culture that manufacturers and retailers became part of the phenomenon. During the early 1950s, the A.B. Coddington Garment Company of LaPorte, Indiana, a manufacturer of women's sportswear, began producing a cream-colored skirt labeled "The Original Senior Cord Skirt" (see Figure 10). Coddington continued manufacturing the cord skirt through 1970 (Coddington). For a number of years, Resneck's Department Store in Marion, Indiana, encouraged "Prize Winning" cord designs by sponsoring an annual Senior Cord Contest (see Figure 11).

Cords were always cords; that is, they were always made of corduroy fabric. Colors ranged from khaki between the 1920s and 1940s, to cream, off-white and light yellow through the 1970s. Two schools, however, varied from the color norms. Women's cords at Purdue University were gold (Viola) and all senior cords at Gavitt High School in Hammond, Indiana, were light blue (Wilson).

Senior Cord Traditions

The significance of senior cords as a symbol used in rites of passage and intensification is exemplified by many of the traditions surrounding the wearing (or not wearing) of cords. Generally, cords were decorated during the summer before and/or the fall of the senior year. The traditions relating to the first day that cords were worn varied from school to school, but most involved either the first day of school or the first football or basketball game of the year. Cords could be worn on any day of the week in some schools and were worn only on prescribed days at other schools (such as Fridays when school athletic events would take place, see Figure 12). Cords were sometimes worn with other specified items of dress such as letter sweaters, derby hats and canes, and even white "bucks" (shoes).

Cord traditions at Purdue University were perhaps the most involved of any school. Seniors wore their cords for the first time at the opening football game of the season at the Cord Day Parade. Prior to the parade, underclassmen would try to steal each senior's cords (Harlan). To prevent that calamity, seniors would create the definitive hiding place: chimneys, drawers with false bottoms, sewn inside quilts, and even sealed in

Fig. 9. Cord Artist at Work. Photograph from 1960 *Sargasso* (186).

Fig. 10. The Original Senior Cord Skirt. Unpublished photograph by Schlick.

Fig. 11. Senior Cord Contest.
Resneck's Department Store Archives.

Fig. 12. Senior Cords at the Game. Photograph from 1958 *Sargasso* (122).

industrial drums. Generally, the ingenuity of the underclassmen prevailed and the cords were discovered and "stolen."

The last day a senior could wear cords was often the final day of the school term. At Lawrence Central High School, underclassmen would attempt to literally tear the cords off the seniors on the final day (Bice). At other schools, cords became part of class wills: "I, Paul Ooley, do hereby will my senior cords to the junior boys" (*Hornet*).

Many cords were never washed. This tradition was sometimes related to the lack of color-fastness of the decorating medium but more often the tradition existed for its own sake. For instance, as a good luck omen, cords at Bloomfield High School were not washed during the state basketball tournament (Birkemeier). From the 1940s through the 1960s, the overriding theme seemed to be "the dirtier the better" (Harding) "so they would stand in a corner without falling down" (Cox). At Brown County High School, a member of the Class of 1964 was reported to have worn his cords for 180 days straight without washing. A student the following year wore his cords every day of the school year without washing (Birkemeier).

Several high schools allowed underclassmen to wear cords in a color designated for their particular class (Alspaugh; Gallien) such as dark green for freshmen, red for sophomores, and dark blue for juniors. Without exception, however, only *senior cords* could be decorated. The punishment for underclassmen wearing senior cords varied. Perhaps the most dramatic punishment was that of physically removing the cords from the unqualified wearer ("depantsing") and running the cords up a flagpole or depositing the offending person in the local creek.

The Demise of Senior Cords

"I am a great believer in tradition and it's a shame if senior cords are no longer a part of the school scene" (Harlan). Rituals and traditions tend to survive within a conservative setting and seem to decline when faced with the liberal force of change. Such was the destiny for senior cords. During the 1960s and early 1970s, several factors contributed to the demise of senior cords. School systems were consolidating resulting in the elimination of local traditions such as senior cords. Society in general began to question its involvement in traditions, ceremonies and rituals. Students were becoming more outspoken and found that they could step beyond the social norms by expressing themselves on their cords. Some seniors took advantage of the situation and included rude and suggestive phrases or illustrations on their cords (see Figure 13), resulting in a ban on cords by the school administrators. In general, small schools in small towns tended to keep the tradition alive longer.

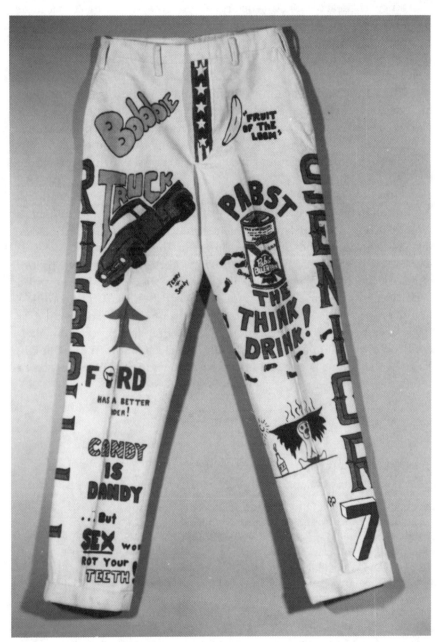

Fig. 13. Senior Cords: Shoals High School, Class of 1971. Unpublished photograph by Schlick.

Since the early 1980's, society has begun returning to a more conservative posture; many rituals and traditions have been reinstated. Purdue University and several high schools have attempted to revive the senior cord tradition but the success of these revivals is yet to be seen.

The senior cord tradition in Indiana is unique. Most class traditions include some form of personalization. However, few of these ritualistic objects are based totally on personalized inscriptions and illustrations, as are senior cords. Further, there is little evidence of other class dress that provides an opportunity for aesthetic expression while presenting one's social identity.

Although class dress of some sort is a part of every educational institution in the United States, it seems that the phenomenon of Indiana's senior cords is unparalleled in its history, its range and scope of statewide involvement, and its depth of meaning for the participant. "My skirt has been a precious memory" (Hamner). 1"Senior cords were a part of our senior year long remembered" (Arthur). "It was an honor and a privilege as a senior to have and wear these cords" (Pruett). The countless Hoosiers who have saved their cords for twenty, forty, and even sixty years have preserved the memories of their friends, their school, their hometown and their passage into the adult world. These memories remain alive on the corduroy trousers and skirts known affectionately as senior cords.

Works Cited

Alspaugh, Gary. Senior Cord Survey. 31 July 1984. [Reynolds, IN: Reynolds High School, Class of 1956.]

Arbutus. 1906. [Yearbook.] Bloomington, IN: Indiana University.

———. 1912. [Yearbook.] Bloomington, IN: Indiana University.

———. 1913. [Yearbook.] Bloomington, IN: Indiana University.

Arthur, Vicki. Senior Cord Survey. 5 September 1984. [Bloomington, IN: Bloomington High School, Class of 1960].

Aurora. 1962. [Yearbook.] Greentown, IN: Eastern High School.

Bice, Jerry. Senior Cord Survey. 2 July 1984. [Lawrence, IN: Lawrence Central High School, Class of 1961.]

Birkemeier, Carol. Senior Cord Survey. 10 July 1984. [Bloomfield, IN: Bloomfield High School, Class of 1967.]

"Classical Cords—Colorful Cycle," *Red and Blue*. [Kokomo, IN: Kokomo High School.] 10 February 1961: 3.

Clayton, Hugh. Senior Cord Survey. 2 August 1984. [Bloomington, IN: Indiana University, Class of 1941.]

Clensy, Nancy. Senior Cord Survey. 17 July 1984. [Bloomfield, IN: Eastern High School, Class of 1971.]

Coddington, Robert E. Coddington Questionnaire. 10 July 1984.

Cox, George. Senior Cord Survey. 11 July 1984. [Bloomington, IN: Bloomington High School, Class of 1943.]

Eberhart, Homer D. Senior Cord Survey. 4 July 1984. [Bloomington, IN: Indiana University, Class of 1926.]

Elliott, Janet. Senior Cord Survey. 24 July 1984. [Paoli, IN: Paoli High School, Class of 1965.]

Flugel, J. C. *The Psychology of Clothes*. New York: International Universities, 1971.

Fox, Robert F. Senior Cord Survey. 3 October 1984. [Washington, IN: Washington High School, Class of 1960.]

Hamner, Millie. Senior Cord Survey. 27 July 1984. [Shelbyville, IN: Southwestern High School, Class of 1965.]

Harding, Joyce. Senior Cord Survey. 8 August 1984. [Bloomington, IN: Bloomington High School, Class of 1959.]

Harlan, Gene. Senior Cord Survey. 23 July 1984. [West Lafayette, IN: Purdue University, Class of 1948.]

Hiam, Jennie. Senior Cord Survey. 28 July 1984. [Hartford City, IN: Hartford City High School, Class of 1959.]

Hornet. 1960. [Yearbook.] Solsberry, IN: Solsberry High School.

Indian. 1943. [Yearbook.] Anderson, IN: Anderson High School.

The Jordannus. 1952 [Yearbook.] Bloomington, IN: University High School.

Kaiser, Susan B., *The Social Psychology of Clothing and Personal Adornment*. New York: MacMillan, 1985.

Kirby, Pat. Senior Cord Survey. 3 July 1984. [Sullivan, IN: Sullivan High School, Class of 1958.]

Lurie, Alison. *The Language of Clothes*. 1981. New York: Vintage, 1983.

McCoy, Anne. Letter to the author. 2 July, 1984.

Owl. 1968. [Yearbook.] Bloomfield, IN: Bloomfield High School.

Pruett, Pat. Letter to the author. 1 August 1984.

Resneck, Dan. Letter to the author. 3 October 1984.

Roach, Mary Ellen and Joanne Bubolz Eicher. *Dress, Adornment, and the Social Order*. New York: John Wiley, 1965.

Rowold, Kathleen Laurie. "Clothing Behavior in Relation to Rites of Passage: Eschatology and Funeral Garb." Diss. Purdue University, 1979.

Sargasso. 1957. [Yearbook.] Kokomo, IN: Kokomo High School.

_____ 1958. [Yearbook.] Kokomo, IN: Kokomo High School.

_____ 1959. [Yearbook.] Kokomo, IN: Kokomo High School.

_____ 1960. [Yearbook.] Kokomo, IN: Kokomo High School.

_____ 1961. [Yearbook.] Kokomo, IN: Kokomo High School.

Schlick, Pamela J. [Unpublished photographs.] Bloomington, IN: Sage Costume Collection, 1985.

Silhouette. 1956. [Yearbook.] Plainfield, IN: Plainfield High School.

Spangler, Norma. Senior Cord Survey. 13 September 1984. [Bloomington, IN: University High School, Class of 1949.]

Szwec, Linda. Senior Cord Survey. 7 July 1984. [North Salem, IN: North Salem High School, Class of 1962.]

Viola, Nancy. Senior Cord Survey. 27 July 1984. [West Lafayette, IN: Purdue University, Class of 1959.]

Wallace, Leon. Letter to the author. 30 July 1984.

Warner, W.L. "The City of the Dead," *Death and Identity*. Ed. R. L. Fulton. New York: John Wiley, 1965.

Wichems, Carol. Letter to the author. 29 June 1984.

Wigwam. 1959. [Yearbook.] Indianapolis, IN: Warren Central High School.

Wilson, Pat. Senior Cord Survey. 4 July 1984. [Hammond, IN: Gavit High School, Class of 1967.]

Young, Dorothy. Letter to the author. 9 September 1984.

The Bicycle, the Bloomer
and Dress Reform in the 1890s

Sally Sims

In the spring of 1900, John B. Tillinghast, on a visit to Washington, D.C., posted a letter to his Uncle Walter:

> I reckon this is the finest city in the world for automobiles and there are hundreds of them here. They just cut about among the horses and street cars with much more ease than you could guide a spirited team. The 'mobiles all have rubber tires and only make a little whirring sound—so you have to watch for them at crossings—although they have a bell like a street car.
> One of them like to got me at one of the big circles as I was crossing the "open"—a policeman had to holler at me. I would have seen it ordinarily but I was watching one of those short-skirted girls get on a wheel—not very interesting probably but I just had a curiosity to see her start off...(Tillinghast)

Tillinghast's letter reflects the tremendous changes in transportation which had occurred by the turn of the century, but his fascination with the woman he saw cycling in the busy streets of Washington is a revealing slice of social history. The 1890s had been a period in which the bicycle was made available to women, and that decade was marked by lively debate over whether women should ride bicycles and, if so, how they should dress and "comport" themselves awheel. The "short-skirted girl" of 1900 represented a phenomenon that could still stop traffic after much of the agitation—and there was plenty of it in the 1890s—had subsided, and American women had adopted cycling as a favorite tonic and means of transport.

Two technological developments were instrumental in bringing together American women and the bicycle in the late 1880s. These were the invention in 1888 of the pneumatic tire,[1] which reduced the jolting caused by solid tires and made cycling more enjoyable for both men and women; and the patenting of the drop-frame safety bicycle (Cunnington and Mansfield 228). Without a crossbar, and with two wheels of equal size, the drop-frame, patented in 1887, was similar to a women's bicycle of today. It caused less interference with a woman's cumbersome skirts than either a high-wheeled "ordinary" or a "diamond frame" (man's) safety bicycle (Palmer 94). Until the advent of the drop-frame safety, and unless she wished to risk derision and caricature, a woman who wanted to ride usually elected to sit alongside her escort in a "sociable"—a tricycle wide enough for two—or to take a spin on a tandem tricycle, whose front seat "nearly always is...adapted to the use of a lady" (Porter 166, 168; McGonagle 88-89).

Although the date of her ride is obscure, Mrs. W. E. Smith was the first woman generally acknowledged to have ridden a safety bicycle "right out in public." Her long, dark skirt, matching jacket and cap constituted a fine outfit for a city jaunt (Browne 65-80). It is not known whether Mrs. Smith met with any public opposition to her appearance on a bicycle. Of greater interest, however, are the many articles in medical journals, popular magazines and cycling handbooks of the 1890s, responding to the steady increase in the popularity of cycling for women. Clearly, middle-class women had taken up this newly available pastime because it released them from the cares of the home and offered healthful exercise. But what would be the effect of such an activity on woman as wife, mother, homemaker? A more troubling issue, in an age of great concern with race progress and social Darwinism, was whether the physical strain of cycling would affect women's childbearing abilities. The medical profession's ultimate endorsement of cycling was based in part on the rationale that woman's role in achieving a superior race type could be enhanced by regular use of the bicycle (Merington 703; Neesen 78-9; Hobson and Winston 84-5).

It was the subject of dress for the bicycle which drew the greater proportion of comment among observers of the day. Discussions about the correct cycling garb were not left solely to the fashion pages of women's magazines. The matter of a suitable bicycling dress for women was symbolic of the question of the suitability of bicycling itself, and became fair game for physicians, critics of the popular scene, and other commentators and wordsmiths. Eventually, society came to recognize that women would dress differently when they rode bicycles and that their dress was, after all, appropriate. As expressed in *Demorest's Family Magazine*, the sight of a woman on a bicycle somehow passed "the period of hysterical and hyperbolic writing with reference to the good or ill effects and the propriety or iniquity." Nevertheless, through the middle years of the decade, woman's cycling dress remained "a much discussed question" (Demorest's 32:465).

To many minds, the wheelwoman of the 1890s was synonymous with the "Bloomer Girl" (Bicycle Mfgs. Assn. 1974). This image has persisted to the present day, and with some reason. Society's shocked reaction to seeing women on bicycles in "bifurcated" or "rational" garments was widely reported in the popular literature (Smith 87). Advertisers capitalized on the image of the "Bloomer Girl" to promote

Fig. 1 A bicycle party of highwheelers; the one woman in the group rides a tricycle which does not require her to straddle the seat. 1887. Source: Library of Congress 47313/262-1243.

Fig. 2 Bicycle party on Riverside Drive, NY. The women in the group sport a variety of bicycling garb. Mid '90s. Source: Library of Congress 14040/262-02114.

products completely unrelated to the bicycle; and cartoons, poems and songs exist which have perpetuated the notion of the carefree female, in a short gathered trouser, astride her shiny wheel. On another, perhaps more serious, and distinctly more positive level, the notion of the "Bloomer Girl" suggested the possibility that cycling would bring about dress reform. It is evident that certain efforts to "improve" woman's dress were connected with or at least influenced by the new and varied costumes available to the woman cyclist. The dress reform movement itself, however, led by Frances E. Russell of St. Paul, Minnesota, operated from its own platform, and bicycling played a related, but indirect, part in its program.

The men and women who expressed themselves on the subject of woman's demeanor, costume and movement on a bicycle had a strong collective sense of socio-economic class obligation. Those who believed cycling to be worthwhile and socially acceptable urged exemplary decorum, for men, certainly, but especially for women on the wheel. Both the women who wrote about and rode bicycles and those who participated in the dress reform movement in the 1890s recognized fully that impeccable personal conduct was the key to gaining and maintaining public favor for either of these interests. Applied to dress, this meant wearing an outfit perhaps unconventional but not deliberately meant to offend, and adapted to the needs of the wearer. Whether these needs were the freedom of the limbs for cycling, or the same freedom and comfort for the everyday routines of a woman's life, the clothing should be entirely modest and *pro forma*. It was within these limits, well marked out along class lines, that certain dress styles effected by the bicycle were accepted as "fitting habiliment" for the woman cyclist of the 1890s (White 225).

And what of the most notable cycling garment of the decade, the bloomer? Outlandish or sensible, mannish or natty, the acme of comfort or downright ugly, it clearly stood out, and continues to do so, as a curious symbol of the 1890s, the heyday of the wheelwoman. As an item of fashion it was equivocal; as a statement of independence it was more so, censured as it finally was by derision and the dictates of fashion. Its very existence, however; its rise and demise on the tides of popular and fashion-world reaction and the state of the bicycle industry itself; had wider ramifications in the continued attempts, throughout the decade and beyond, to resolve the disturbing questions surrounding women's dress, duties and direction.

Physicians and Fashion: What to Wear Awheel?

As tricycling preceded bicycling as an outdoor amusement for women, so also did the fashion pages of women's magazines first feature "cycling gowns" intended to be worn on the tricycle. The first such dress shown in *Demorest's Family Magazine* varied little from everyday dress of the time, save for extra fullness in the skirt and through the back (32:468). The limited locomotion provided by the tricycle was perfectly reflected in this fairly confining costume. Tricyling dress, though, drew little significant attention from observers in the medical, fashion or popular press. The strenuousness of bicycling, the "sweeping" motions of the limbs, and the relationship between this startling physical activity and women's dress caused a far greater reaction from all manner of writers on the subject (Townsend 595).

Women cyclists themselves wrote feelingly of the joys of their newfound pastime. *The Wheelwoman,* a magazine whose first issues immediately preceded the peak of bicycle production in 1896, catered enthusiastically to the middle-class female cycling trade with rhapsodic accounts by new "converts" as well as with displays of the latest equipage for the cyclist and her mount. Both the cycle and its accoutrements were expensive, even by today's standards, and quite out of reach of lower-income consumers (Campbell 139-40).

In contrast to women cyclists' own lyric celebration of the wheel, certain medical men expressed great alarm and discomposure over the potential effects on women's bodies of bicycling. Dr. James A. Roosevelt in 1895 referred to "certain anatomical and physiological peculiarities which make it far more dangerous for a woman than for a man to undergo excessive physical strain" (Roosevelt 712). Doctors also warned, more logically, of the harmful effects of constricting bands: "Tight garters, of course, come under the ban; and the stiff, choker collar should be banished with the tightly laced corset" (*Demorest's* 32:468).

Of all these confining garments, it was the corset to which writers on this subject directed the most attention. Dr. Victor Neesen laid out the grim effects of wearing tight corsets while exercising:

The stomach and spleen are pushed upward and backward, against the heart, interfering with its action. The liver is pressed upon and pushed upward, diminishing the space in which the lungs expand. The intestines are crowded down on the pelvic organs, which are liable to be displaced, and the pressure on the large vessels causes a stagnation of blood in the valveless veins of the sexual organs—a potent cause of many of the ailments peculiar to women.(68)

It was its tightness, however, which was said to do the most harm, and not the wearing of the garment itself. The "narrow string" of constriction caused by the waistband of a skirt might be more dangerous than the "diffuse pressure" of a corset (Neesen 69). Dr. Charles W. Townsend recommended "short corsets which do not press on the abdomen," or the "comfortable, loose 'health' waists," firm, waist-length foundations without bones or steels (594). Some form of trunk support was thought not only necessary but "a decided improvement to almost every figure." Only women who "from their youth up" had never worn corsets—and who were they?—ought to set out on a bicycle ride without them (Porter 111).

It is important to note the conflicting lines of thought about woman's health and her beauty, in relation to dress and physical activity. Not only was it assumed that women ought to wear corsets. In the face of evidence that wearing them might impair women's ability to reproduce, doctors still readily conceded that the corseted figure of a woman was really most attractive. Was the question, then, one of the relative delicacy of the female body, or of society's preference that women maintain the role of parlor ornament? If it was necessary for women to be fit enough to bring forth a strong and hardy race, should doctors not be concerned that corseted muscles of otherwise healthy women were atrophying from disuse (Caird 63)?

Still, the introduction of the health corset—sometimes even referred to as a bicycle waist—had to be looked on as a step, if only a small one, toward an improved standard of dress for women. With the modified foundation could be worn "no end of...shirts...[which] are loose and comfortable," advised Dr. Neesen, as he added knowingly, "tight clothes are impossible on the wheel" (*Wheelwoman* 3:215).

As to the outer garments, the ensemble which Dr. Neesen recommended was telling in its simple wholesomeness and particularly in its designation of a "short" skirt:

1. Union garment of silk or thin wool.
2. Equestrian tights from knee to waist, or bloomers
   [as underwear] same as for men.
3. Stockings.
4. High boots.
5. Shirt waist or woolen waist.
6. Short [four to eight inches above the ground] skirt.
7. Eton or Luey [short, tailored] jacket.
8. Alpine, Derby, Straw or Tam O'Shanter Hat (Neesen 69).

The costume to strive for was always "neat," "natty," or "trig." Full sleeves were not desirable; they might detract from the cut of an otherwise "trig" costume and would be distracting if they whipped in the wind (Korns 25). Plain colors were designated, but might vary as to taste and practicality: "Tan and brown and fine mixed cloths of these prevailing tones have been proved by experience to be a much better choice for cycling...than black and blue, [which] show the dust so, and soon grow brown and shabby." (*Demorest's* 32:467)

The controversy brought on by the bicycling skirt—particularly its length—was as cumbersome as the garments which "trig"- and comfort-minded persons sought to discard. L.F. Korns, for one, would have none of the short skirt, placing full responsibility on the rear wheel dress guard of a women's bicycle to prevent any inconvenience caused by a bulky garment. Korns suggested that the only alternative to the long skirt must be the purely nonsensical pantaloon costume which she presented in her cycling handbook (24-5).

Writer R. L. Dickinson decreed the long skirt, two inches off the ground, to be the only one approved by fashion and the most generally advantageous:

For the woman who is too thin, for the leisurely rider in fair weather, and for the woman shy of comment, it gives a suitable garb, together with that comfort which conformity brings. Its convenience at present is that the cyclist can step off her wheel into the shop or house and be clad as her uniformed sisters are (751).

Both Korns and Dickinson were women, and their firm preference for long skirts was notable. Their writings represented that given law of the woman awheel: To convince others of the benefits of the bicycle, women riders must maintain an even pace and a pleasant aspect. To Korns and Dickinson, this meant wearing a costume which barely deviated from current modes in daytime dress.

The tone of much of the writing by women on the subject of dress and behavior on the wheel was usually good-humored and rather sportive, save for the ever-present reminder not to over-exert. An interview in the August 1896 *Wheelwoman* with journalist Marion Howard Brazier described how Brazier "from an Opponent Becomes an Enthusiast":

"I ride in moderation...the main thing is to keep up a proper circulation, a ladylike speed, and erect seat, and have congenial friends alongside. Costume? Well, I do not believe with some who cross our vision that 'any old thing will do to wear on a wheel,' neither do I see the necessity of a woman unsexing herself in hideous bloomers. The fewer clothes the better,—a moderately short skirt, everything trig and well-fastened, and laced boots. Flower-laden hats and flying coat-tails are an abomination" (3:6).

By the close of the 1890s shortened skirts, as recommended by Brazier, had gained acceptance as the best cycling dress for women. (*Vanity Fair* 1:27). As *Demorest's* announced in 1896, the outcome of the heated debates of the previous seasons was "what all sensible people expected: that the majority of women would adopt a modest, becoming, and convenient manner of dressing, with sufficient variety to individualize it." (294)

Before the achievement of this plateau, however, various interested parties were offering ways to deal with the long skirt on the bicycle. Luther Henry Porter's book described a system of shortening a long skirt by "providing it with four straps, arranged to look like ornaments, and hanging at equal intervals from the waist. A short distance below each strap is a button, to which it can be attached," and thus pull the skirt up approximately six inches from the floor (109). Drawing from his wife's experience, Porter maintained, a skirt "of ordinary walking length, not too full, and of fairly heavy material, even for summer use" ought to preclude the "difficulties and dangers that have beset women's skirts...due to...too great length, too much fullness, or too light material" (107-109). An article titled "Bicycling Riding for Women" which appeared in *Outlook* in 1895 described the "safety" technique of turning up a four-to-five-inch hem on the skirt and securing it with ten rows of machine stitching to stiffen it and prevent its tangling in the wheel. The skirt was to come to the ankle (51:1104).

At the other extreme from the heavy skirt, and the various tricks and contraptions designed to keep it in place, were two garments. They were the divided skirt,[2] "so fastened that it hangs in the form and shape of a regular skirt, but in reality so divides as to facilitate the movement of the rider's limbs," and, of course, the bloomer (Porter 112-13). The divided skirt was admittedly convenient for mounting a bicycle. Because of its fullness, however, it was, if more than eight inches above the ground, "extremely liable to blow up above the knees, when it looks worse and attracts more attention than to ride without a skirt" (*Demorest's* 32:46). Moreover, protested *The Wheelwoman*, divided skirts hardly ever hung well except when the wearer sat astride her wheel. At other times, such as when walking a bicycle up a hill, "the divided skirts are too ugly for words" (3:214). As Henry Clyde, author of *Pleasure Cycling*, concluded in 1895, "the 'divided skirt' appears already to be relegated to the limbo of ugly absurdities...It is certain," he prophesied, "that women on the wheel will generally wear either absolute trousers or absolute skirts" (135).

The absolute trouser, then, better known as the knickerbocker, rational garment, or bloomer; full-legged, gathered at the knee, and worn with the same hat, leggins and jacket that comprised any trig cycling costume, was the subject of much consideration (and ventilation!) for about two seasons, from 1895 to 1897. This was the peak of the bicycling craze. As the bloomer burst on the fashion scene in 1895, it was initially portrayed as a viable form of bicycle dress for women (Gernsheim 80). This is not to suggest that it had not been seen or written of earlier in the decade; the bloomer was, however, a strong "fashion item" in the women's magazines of 1895-1896.

The name *bloomer* derived from the early proponent of the garment, Amelia Jenks Bloomer. In 1851, Elizabeth Smith Miller was visiting her cousin, woman suffrage leader Elizabeth Cady Stanton, in Seneca Falls, New York, where Bloomer also lived. It was Miller who introduced the "rational" costume to Bloomer, who in turn wrote of it in her temperance magazine, *The Lily*. From there the interest spread. The bloomer costume of the 1850s consisted of a tunic dress over long trousers, which were gathered at the ankle. The full-legged knickerbocker of the 1890s took its form from the loose undergarments which preceded it, and from men's sporting garments of that time, and its name from the 1850s form (Bloomer, 70-3). Ultimately, according to *Vanity Fair* in 1896, it was scorned and jeered as it passed out of favor with "fashion's votaries" (1:116).

Some women who cycled discovered a method of having the advantages of both skirt and bloomer. They managed this by wearing a skirt over a bloomer of the same fabric. Once a woman was out on the country road, beyond civilization's watchful eye, she could remove the skirt and ride in just the matching bloomer. As she approached town again, she would put the skirt back on (*Demorest's* 32:466).

The obvious next step was to dispense with the skirt altogether.

"The advantages of bloomers are considerable," Luther Henry Porter allowed.

They offer less resistance to the wind; there is more freedom in the use of the limbs; there is nothing to catch in the machine in mounting, dismounting, or in riding; chain and wheel guards can be removed from the machine altogether, or a diamond frame [man's] wheel can be used if desired.(116-17)

The life span of the bloomer was short, however. In 1896 *Demorest's* remarked that "their use without a skirt is confined to a very small minority, and it cannot be said that they have gained any ground in the past year" (32:466).

Ironically, *The Wheelwoman* itself, which had come into being with the popularity of cycling for women, loudly echoed the bloomer's death knell. The grounds on which the garment was condemned were, characteristically, its "unwomanliness" and its association with a social group not of "that class of people who compose what is known as society and who set the fashions." " 'Waving of banners and a flare of trumpets!' is too tame an expression to use in describing its advent,...but the bloomer never did reign" (4:395-96). "Women drew distinct lines," observed a reporter from *Cycling Gazette*, "and no person in bloomers could hope to enter a fashionable club or house" (*Wheelwoman* 3:5). As Mary Sargent Hopkins, *The Wheelwoman*'s editor, paraphrased, "The bloomer and knickerbocker have come, seen, but by no means conquered" (4:329).

The coming woman of a few years ago has passed into history—the skirt has won and man's wardrobe is safe...That advance movement in female dress which had no end in view has been checked and made to beat a disorderly retreat.(3:214)

The world has bid farewell to the garb which never should have been, and is making great and glorious the reign of the queen of costumes...The wheel has undoubtedly caused common sense to be used in the fashioning of skirts, but it signally failed in its attempt to abolish them or even limit their use.(4:396)

Viewed as a "sensible, if not aesthetic garment," *Vanity Fair* noted, the bloomer costume could be considered one of a range of outfits available to the woman cyclist, but one whose fashion interest never developed beyond the status of a mild eccentricity (1:116). Viewed, on the other hand, as the "awful bloomer," something to be "extinguished altogether," its import took on vastly different proportions (*Wheelwoman* 3:5). It was a (male) voice in the wilderness which cried, "Why should [a woman] not mount her wheel like a man, and, like a man, enjoy all possible freedom of movement" that trousers would offer her (Clyde 134-35)? Why? For the same underlying reasons that caused physicians to temper their endorsements of cycling, and for men and women alike to call for an upright, neatly-dressed woman awheel. They anxiously observed the bloomer's short-lived period of fashion and breathed relief as it faded out of vogue. It was utterly mind-boggling to consider the consequences of women's becoming used to wearing trousers in public.

Thus the shortened skirt saved the day in several respects. Compared to longer skirts it was indeed safer and more comfortable. According to the *Wheelwoman*, it allayed the fears of those who foresaw the masculinization of female America via the creeping efforts of that "advance movement in dress" (3: 214). But whether or not by the conscious effort of some such movement, the public, because of the bicycle, became accustomed to seeing women in skirts a full eight inches above the ground (3:264).

"Rainy Day" and Rational Costume: The Bicycle and Dress Reform

Although not usually discussed in these terms in contemporary writings, the adoption of the shortened skirt for bicycling, and the use of modified, more flexible corsets, signaled a new concept, the specialization of women's clothing for certain activities. Individuals who had looked to the bicycle as a coming agent of women's dress reform could rightly be pleased with this accomplishment. While it reinforced a widening recognition that women could and would participate in activities outside the home, the bicycle also called some attention to sex-distinction in work, recreation and dress. At the same time, the "sensible" wearing of the shortened skirt acted as an emollient to the raw nerves of society which the bloomer had exposed.

The eventual stabilization of the question of women's bicycle dress ran a different course from that of dress reform as such. Dr. Neesen, in enumerating the long-range advantages of wheeling, did look to "an epoch toward which the female world has been struggling for a century,"

2332—" Sew on your own buttons, I'm going for a ride."

Fig. 3 Everyman's Fear: The wife leaves him with chores and children! 1899. Source: Library of Congress 14040/62-50832.

Fig. 4 March-Davis Admiral advertisement, 1897. The classic, acceptable "trig" costume of the late '90s. Note the wheel guard on the rear wheel. Source: Library of Congress 14040/262-28612.

the day when woman would "wear a more hygienic dress," discarding "too heavy and too tight clothing" (79). The doctor's allusion was somewhat vague, however, and not immediately connected with the formal agenda of the dress reform movement. Yet as society became inured to the shorter skirt for cycling, proponents of that "more hygienic dress" were beginning to see this revised cycling costume as a true catalyst to improve women's clothing. B.O. Flower of the socially alert *Arena*, observed a strong concern not only with weighty and confining garments, but especially with muddy hems and germ-ridden roadways, had prompted the formation in Boston of a "Rainy Day Club" early in the 1890s. Both B. O. Flower, and Mary Sargent Hopkins, editor of *The Wheelwoman*, greeted the new organization with wholehearted approval. As Hopkins declared,

In taking her place beside man in the breadwinning contest of life, a woman must subject herself to many changes if she would win success. The exigencies of professional or business life which take women out of doors in all weathers call for a radical change in her attire (3:264).

Shortened skirts for business and professional wear, at least in foul weather, was the goal of the (un-named) "doctors, literary women, reporters, and business women of high standing" who were the members of the Club. *The Wheelwoman* observed that these women had pledged not only to help other women make over old skirts for rainy-day wear, but also to request employers to approve and permit the wearing of such skirts. (3:265) Hopkins, writing in the *Wheelwoman* in 1896, was convinced that the Rainy Day Club's success had been due almost solely to the wide acceptance of the shortened bicycle skirt:

"Street dress," "walking skirts," "rainy day costume," never would have appealed to us as has "bicycle suit," which not only had an appropriateness all its own, but which was adaptable to all outdoor occasions. Then, too, the freedom that women found in riding the wheel, naturally led them to question whether the enjoyment they found in their short skirts could not be applied in other ways (3:264).

The Rainy Day Club, brought to life by the wheel, did set certain guidelines for selection of raiment which were published in the *Wheelwoman*:

No great good could be accomplished unless the costume be one that the most particular husband, father or brother could see nothing to object to...

Nothing must be worn that could...in any way make the wearer look other than a self-respecting, womanly woman (3:265).

According to these principles, the woman of the 1890s, if she wished to modify her dress in any way, had three apparent alternatives: She could dress as a woman, as the sexless clown L. F. Korns had presented, or as a man. On the other hand, she could *dress* as either the second or the third and continue to conduct herself in a "womanly" way. To most women this latter notion would have been ridiculous. How could dress change—if that was really so desirable—take place, maintain woman's self-respect, and avoid offending husband, father, brother? Frances E. Russell, who chaired the Symposium on Dress of the National Council of Women in 1892 and 1893, believed that it could be done ("Freedom" 76).[3] According to Russell, the aim of her committee was to achieve acceptance of a new everyday "business dress" for women, and the members offered three basic models, each to be worn with a short jacket. [The 1893 Symposium had the following members: Frances E. Russell, of St. Paul, who since her first reading of a dress reform tract thirty-six years before had done much writing and study on the subject; Frances M. Steele, a founder of the Chicago Society for the Promotion of Physical Culture and Correct Dress; Mrs. E. M. King, a founder of the English Rational Dress Society; Elizabeth Smith Miller, cousin of Elizabeth Cady Stanton, and first to wear the bloomer costume in the 1850s; Octavia W. Bates, "an admirable representative of the college-trained woman of the progressive type"; and dress-reform advocates Annie Jenness Miller, Grace Greenwood, and Dr. Mary Emery ("Symposium" 488-507).] The models included the "Syrian" which had a divided skirt, gathered around each ankle; the "English" which was divided just above the knees, with wide legs; and the "American" which had narrow trousers ("Freedom" 76). Even as Otis Tufton Mason, Curator of the Department of Ethnology in the Smithsonian, was preparing a justification of the wearing of skirts by women through his study of American, African, Polynesian and Australian tribes (237), Russell, in a history of dress reform efforts published in the *Arena* in 1892, had traced the wearing of a divided garment to the women of Biblical times:

The nether garment was first worn in bifurcated form by the women of ancient Judah...The exclusive claim which men so pertinaciously maintain to the use of this garment, is founded upon no principle of moral or social policy...Nature never intended that the sexes be distinguished by apparel ("American" 336).

With this philosophy in mind the members of Russell's symposium wore examples of the costumes they had developed to the World's Columbian Exposition in Chicago in 1893. Both at the fair and during the course of their daily business, the women reported, the response to their clothing was quite favorable; some persons who stopped to comment even requested the patterns for the garments (Russell, "Rational" 322-23). The members agreed that it was only the ill-bred individual who

THE SYRIAN DRESS.

Fig. 5 This dress is recommended by the Rational Dress Society of London. It is a costume adopted from the Orient, and is said by those who have worn it to be "at once graceful and delightfully comfortable." The organ of the Rational Dress Society states that "It is perfectly easy to make, being the simplest form of skirt ever introduced. Of course the fact that the skirt is dual is obvious." Source: Arena v.6 (1892) p. 642.

would publicly deprecate this new form of dress. If faced with such a situation, one must hold one's head high and carry on (Russell, "Rational" 307).

The members of the Symposium on Dress came to a point, however, at which they wore rational garments less frequently, or ceased wearing them altogether, in favor of standard dress. Amelia Bloomer, who had espoused rational dress forty years earlier, explained that she and others had seen the necessity to abandon rational dress if they wished to pursue the rights of women on a broader scale. Reform costume was too greatly entwined with women's rights to make an impact on its own, and it also sometimes alienated potential supporters of the larger causes (Bloomer 72-3). Frances Russell, speaking for the Symposium, responded candidly to the disappointment dress reform advocates felt as the movement declined in momentum:

They [those interested in dress reform] had many different duties and diplomatic relations, and in this latter-day campaign, no one is asked to make a martyr of herself...What we seek especially is a wide awakening and an impetus of numbers, so that those who want the freedom of their limbs may find liberty and not social ostracism. ("American" 307)

To the extent that dress reform philosophy was directed toward and essentially confined to educated, middle-class women, it continued to be governed by particular definitions of womanly behavior, and thus that much more limited in its impact. It challenged the very class from which it emerged and forfeited a unity with other women, thereby unpropitiously spiting itself.

It was the quality of being middle-class in availability and popularity which made bicycling, especially for women, subject to some of the same standards and limitations that the dress reform movement endured. The rule of the "queen of costumes" over the masculine bloomer was frank evidence of this, as were the clear expectations that commentators had of the wheelwoman as American Woman. The writer in *The Wheelwoman* who cheered the exit of the "awful bloomer" shooed it from the fashion stage altogether by asserting, rather horridly, "No woman can endure contempt long, whether she knows she is right or wrong" (3: 5).

The grand reinstatement of the ruling member of female fashion occurred at just about the point when the bicycle market, after a fairly steady increase, began its marked decline. Although prices had been falling since 1894, sales held steady until 1896.[4] It was only then that the bicycle was realistically available to the masses, having previously been the almost exclusive province of the middle-class customer. Women's dress for the bicycle had by this time run its course as a vital issue in the American bourgeois press, whose writers had little interest in the behavior of persons "outside society."

Fig. 6 Pope CHAINLESS model advertisement, 1904. Even with a changing silhouette, a shorter skirt is maintained. Note the shoes and hat are not suitable for sporting activity. Source: *Frank Leslie's Popular Monthly*, 1904.

Throughout the first half of the decade there was much vocalizing on the subject of the proper costume for the woman awheel, and a good deal of speculation as to whether the new modes for cycling might lead to changes in women's dress across the board. Meanwhile, the dress reform movement had stirred women to consider the advantages of alternative garments for business and professional wear, as more and more of them stepped out of the home and into the working world, complete with its germ-laden roadways. Their outfits, and those of some wheelwomen, raised eyebrows in their time. Soon enough, those who had experimented with rational dress and bloomers displaced these with skirts—wisely chosen, their wearers believed, to counter excess criticism. Whether the wheelwoman were a member of "society" or, as prices of bicycles declined, a wage laborer, she was affected in the long run by the strength of middle-class values which encouraged her to stick close, even in casual recreation, to the fashion forms of the day.

Although the bloomer had a brief and maladjusted life on the wheel, it survived long enough to reveal that some women were bold or self-confident or simply comfort-minded enough to wear such garments. In turn, the aura of "masculinization" was strong enough to erode whatever degree of good feeling had accompanied the wearing of the bloomer costume. The shortened skirt, of course, became the best evidence of all that the majority of women had no intention of becoming "defeminized" by that bifurcated garment.

Women would, however, adapt their clothing to their needs, and this was a most positive statement of the wheelwoman of the 1890s. As Mary Sargent Hopkins would verify, the pleasant connotations of wheeling were a partial foundation for such organizations as the Rainy Day Club, and set the stage for the relaxation of women's dress in the century to come. The challenge was for women to convince other women that changes could and should be made, for their benefit as human beings.

Notes

[1]Archibald Sharp credited James Dunlop as the inventor of the pneumatic tire, as did Cunnington and Mansfield. Sharp, however, dated the invention to 1890 (Sharp).

[2]Although Robert E. Riegel in "Women's Clothes and Women's Rights" asserted that divided skirts became extremely popular during the bicycle craze, contemporary evidence is to the contrary (390-401).

[3]Another important advocate of modifications in women's dress in the 1890s was Helen Gilbert Ecob. Ecob concentrated more on the aesthetics of dress than did other writers, and she favored loose, flowing gowns. Waist-binding was to Ecob the greatest evil of dress. (Ecob).

[4]The average price of a fully equipped and assembled bicycle fell in 1894 from $150 to $125, then in 1895 to $100 (United States 30). By the fall of 1897, the *Sears,*

Roebuck Catalog featured bicycles at $29.90 and, by the following spring, in the $13.95 and $19.95 price range (Spring, 1897:485, Fall, 1898: 412-13).

Works Cited

Bicycle Manufacturers Association of America, Inc. *History of the Bicycle.* Washington and New York: 1974.

"Bicycle Riding for Women," *Outlook* 1895: 1104.

Bloomer, Dexter. *Life and Writing of Amelia Jenks Bloomer.* Boston: *Arena*, 1895.

Browne, Herbert Janvrin. "Athletics in Washington," *Outing* 1890: 65-80.

Caird, Mona Alison. *The Morality of Marriage and Other Essays on the Status and Destiny of Woman.* London: G. Redway, 1897.

Campbell, Helen Stuart. *Women Wage-earners: Their Past, Their Present, and Their Future.* Boston: Roberts, 1893.

Clyde, Henry. *Pleasure-Cycling.* Boston: Little, Brown, 1895.

Cunnington, Phillis and Alan Mansfield. *English Costume for Sports and Outdoor Recreation from the Sixteenth to the Nineteenth Centuries.* London: Adam and Charles Black, 1969.

Demorest's Family Magazine. 1896: 294; 465-468.

Dickinson, R. L. "Bicycling for Women: The Puzzling Question of Costume," *Outlook* 1896, 751-752.

Ecob, Helen Gilbert. *The Well-Dressed Woman: A Study in the Practical Application to Dress of the Laws of Health, Art and Morals.* New York: Fowler and Wells, 1893.

Flower, B.O. "Next Forward Step for Women; or, The Movement for Rational Dress," *Arena* October 1892: 635-44.

Gernsheim, Alison. *Fashion and Reality.* London: Faber and Faber, 1963.

Hobson, Florence and Ella W. Winston. "Advice to the New Woman," *Review of Reviews* July 1895: 84-5.

Korns, L. F. *The Bicycle: Its Selection, Riding and Care.* Chicago: L. F. Korns, 1892.

McGonagle, Seamus. *The Bicycle in Life, Love, War and Literature.* London: Pelham, 1968.

Mason, Otis Tufton. *Woman's Share in Primitive Culture.* New York: Appleton, 1894.

Merington, Marguerite. "Woman and the Bicycle," *Scribner's Monthly* June 1895: 702-04.

Neesen, Victor. *Dr. Neesen's Book on Wheeling.* New York: New Amsterdam Book Co., 1899.

Palmer, Arthur Judson. *Riding High: The Story of the Bicycle.* New York: Dutton, 1956.

Porter, Luther Henry. *Cycling for Health and Pleasure.* New York: Dodd, Mead, 1895.

Riegel, Robert E. "Women's Clothes and Women's Rights," *American Quarterly* Fall 1963: 390-401.

Roosevelt, James W. "Doctor's View of Bicycling," *Scribner's Monthly* 1895: 708-12.

Russell, Frances E. "American Dress Reform Movements of the Past, With View of Representative Women," *Arena* Aug. 1892: 325-39.

_____ "Freedom in Dress for Women," *Arena* June 1893: 70-7.

_____ "The Rational Dress Movement," *Arena* Feb. 1893: 305-26.

Sears, Roebuck Catalog. Fall 1897, Spring 1898.

Sharp, Archibald. *Bicycles and Tricycles: An Elementary Treatise on Their Design and Construction.* London and New York: Longmans, Green and Co., 1896.

Smith, Robert A. *A Social History of the Bicycle.* New York: American Heritage, 1972.

"Symposium or Women's Dress," *Arena* 1892: 488-507.

Tillinghast, John B. Letter to Uncle Walter, 16 March 1900, Tillinghast Family Papers, Perkins Library, Duke University. Quoted with permission.

Townsend, Charles W. "Bicycling for Women," *Boston Medical and Surgical Journal* June 1895: 593-95.

United States Bureau of the Census, *Census of Manufactures, 1905: Automobiles, Bicycles and Tricycles.* Bull. no. 66, Washington: G.P.O., 1907.

Vanity Fair. 1896: 27, 116.

Wheelwoman. 1896: 5-6, 214-215; 264-265.

_____ 1897: 329; 395-396.

White, S. P. "Modern Mannish Maidens," *Blackwood's* Feb. 1890: 252-64.

Witches' Weeds

Pat Trautman

You know her: she is old, with bent-over decrepit shape; she has cragged teeth and fingers, and long unkempt hair; sometimes you fancy she has warts and green skin; and she is good with herbs—to perform both good and evil...

You recognize her: by her tall pointed hat with flat brim; by her black and sometimes tattered clothes, and her hooded cloak which has been known to hide unpleasant surprises; by her broom used for travelling to Sabbat and flying about at night; and by her black cat and, perhaps, her yellow birds and black ravens.

We all recognize this witch—the malefic witch—but how? There is no one source which describes or depicts her precisely—nor can there be, for we all know a witch can change her shape at will, favoring black cats and beautiful young maidens. Yet the stereotype is not random or else accusations of witchcraft would have been dismissed by the seventeenth century courts; Nathaniel Hawthorne, Arthur Miller, and L. Frank Baum, among others, would have had to describe her in detail before they could conjure her spirit; and we would not recognize her now. Instead, she is part of our common memory; we are born knowing her.

This essay will look at American witches—real and fictitious— in an attempt to discover how and why we all "know" what witches look like. The discussion commences with New England witches in the seventeenth century, who they were, and why the community thought them to be witches.

I

"The official record of witchcraft in New England belongs entirely to the seventeenth century. In all its unofficial aspects that history would long continue...well into the nineteenth century" (Demos 387). By law, witchcraft in America was punishable by death. No witches were ever burned in this country. However, thirty-six witches were executed in the seventeenth century before the formation of the nation. The best-known episode of witch persecution in New England occurred in 1692 in Salem, Massachusetts when there were 19 executions and three additional deaths attributed to the witchcraft proceedings. During the early colonial period in New England numerous persons were accused of witchcraft. According to Weisman between 1630 and 1692 in Massachusetts Bay alone there were 198 complaints of witchcraft (148 in Salem) with only 5 executions before the Salem episode. Although a few men, generally related to already-accused or suspected witches, found themselves among the accused, the vast majority of complaints were lodged against women. This was so much the case that when one thinks "witch," one automatically assumes "female."

Throughout our national history and continuing to live in our popular literature, these women have been characterized as old, possibly very old, living alone or with spinster daughter(s), who, in some cases, would also be suspected of witchcraft. In other words, they lived on the periphery of the socially acceptable roles—they were past child-bearing years, having produced no surviving male heirs (and thereby stood to inherit larger portions of a spouse's estate); and did not have, nor were dependent upon, a male figure for economic support or social definition. In this manner they were not following society's norms for a patriarchal society and orderly passage of property between generations of men. Whether isolated by choice or circumstance, these women were viewed as self-sufficient, assertive in their rights, in control of their landed property and other economic assets, and a threat to a male-dominated society in their denial to submit to a husband and bear children. Normally there was also noticeable marital friction if the accused was, or had been, married.

The accused witch could come from all social classes yet most often she came from the lower ranks of society, and she was poor. Although some wealthy ladies, such as Governor Phips' wife and some ministers' wives or family members, were accused, they were either not prosecuted or not convicted. In fact, their accusation helped to bring the 1692 craze to a halt. Although members of all social classes could be accused, and were, those whose families were worth under L200—and therefore not members of the elite class according to sumptuary legislation—were overrepresented among those prosecuted. This suggests that economic position may have been more important to the judges trying the cases than to the community as accuser. If an accused were a single-woman with economic resources, that wealth provided a modicum of protection against prosecution (Karlsen 77-80). However, once convicted, all property could be confiscated by the state. All of these circumstances contributed to cementing the community's identification of witches and witchcraft with the lower classes.

Although old age, single status, and either lower socio-economic rank or control of economic assets characterized most of the witches, not all women possessing these traits *were* accused. In addition to societal isolation and no male support or heirs, they also had openly ignored unspoken rules. For example, they took neighbors to court over disagreements (who now retaliated by crying "witch!"); they complained of injustice in distribution of inheritance, about not being allowed full control over property which came to them legitimately; they were able to prosper in business, which made them particularly vulnerable to accusation if a man had been previously unsuccessful in the same endeavor; they were successful midwives, yet had allowed some child to die, which should have lived, while successfully keeping from death others which should not have survived; and they were providers of herbal medicines which could work miracles—or kill. Most likely they were neither members of the Church nor docile, God-fearing Church-goers. Probably they had also foretold events—such as death of another's cows. In New England it was not unusual for there to be a connection made between being a witch and being the cause of some specific harm to someone, most often a close neighbor. In summary, the accused had both overstepped the bounds of "womanly propriety," *and* possessed uncommon knowledge. When a woman demonstrated several of these qualities she became vulnerable to being named a witch (Heyrman 112). Women living alone and over 60 years old were in the most danger of being accused.

Accusations could come many years after an actual incident of bewitchment, and long after any male relatives who might have offered protection had died. Hence, our mental vision of a malefic witch—a poor, old, decrepit woman with poor hygiene, unkempt appearance, long finger nails (for midwifery?) and, maybe, warts, who lived outside the norm of acceptable female behavior.

II

Did these seventeenth-century women wear clothing which set them apart as witches? Did they advertise themselves as such? Even though at first glance the "witch's" hat resembles the seventeenth-century hat, the witches did not wear an outfit which set them apart as such, nor did their clothes resemble our common-memory stereotype of what a witch should be wearing. Furthermore, clothing is not even mentioned as a group affiliation distinguishing feature. After all, since most women initially disclaimed being a witch, why would they dress in a manner which clearly set them apart as one? However, in a few instances clothing *was* described in order to procure positive identification of an accused witch: she was known by a specific outfit which she was known to wear. And all outfits described in the official testimony could have belonged (by sumptuary legislation) to any lower class female, young or old!

Testimony at the Salem witch trials in 1692 reveals that the devil promised to fulfill the dreams of a low status person—he promised prospects of fine clothing, personal power, money, control, and freedom from labor. Trial testimony also is revealing in the manner in which descriptions of dress are used to positively identify the accused. However, they do not mention any specific dress as the badge of witches. That same testimony does nonetheless indicate that even in the seventeenth century brooms, black cats, and yellow birds *were* associated with bewitching capabilities and could be called upon to help prove a person's relationship to witchcraft.

In the case of Bridget Bishop alias Oliver (June 2, 1692) she was identified as *the* witch in question because her coat (*equivalent of a modern-day skirt*) was torn. Samuel Gray (age 42) testified he knew her by her apparel: he recognized her by her "countenance and garb" as the same woman. William Stacy testified that she sat at the foot of his bed and had on a "black cap and a black hat, and a red coat with two [eakes] of two couleurs: then she the said Bishop or her shape clapt here coate close to her leggs and lept upon the bed and about the roome and then went out..." (Boyer and Nissenbaum, vol. 1, 93) Richard Coman (age 32, referring to an incident about eight years previous) stated "Bishop came in her red paragon (*a coarse worsted or camblet used for common wear*) bodys (*bodice without sleeves*) and the rest of her clothing that she then usually did ware, and I knowing of her well also the garb she did use to go in did clearly and plainly know her" (Boyer and Nissenbaum, Vol. 1, 102).

The clothing mentioned is the same as that worn by, and identified with, the lower classes: wool coats and bodices, with red being a preferred color. The elite would have worn gowns, probably of silk. Black caps and hats were popular among all classes, but hatbands would have been a distinguishing feature of the elite, and not missed in a description of apparel meant to convey a positive identification.

Clothing was therefore used to identify the person, but not the person as a witch. If fact, Edward Putnam (age 36) and Ezekiel Cheever (age 37) were to "take good notice of what clothes Goody Cory [the accused] came in that so we might see whither shee [Ann Putnam] was not mistaken in the person." As the story goes, Goody Cory had supposedly blinded Ann Putnum so Ann would not know what she [Goody Cory] wore, and her identification could not be conclusive (Boyer and Nissenbaum, vol. 1, 260). That an accused's clothing was only evidence of her identity and not evidence of her identity as a witch is further substantiated by the fact that there was no one who searched the house for apparel specifically linking her to Satan. Satan himself, however, was repeatedly described as a "black man with a high crowned [*but not pointed*] hat on his head...", suggesting a most specific image of the devil incarnate (plate 1). This could be the kernel of our association of witches' weeds (*clothing, perhaps specific to a profession or stage of life*) with high crowned hats and the color black.

III

If not originating in the seventeenth-century, then when and why did the caftan and/or hooded cloak, and flat brimmed pointed-crown hat develop as witches' weeds? A woodcut dating from 1728 (plate 2) demonstrates the continuing association of witches with lower-class women and their everyday garb—without cloak or hat. Sometime in the second quarter of the nineteenth century, an image of a witch emerged as a female astride a broom, wearing a quilted petticoat, a cloak, and square-toed shoes with Louis heels and buckles from ca. 1776. Her forearms are bare, with the upperarm garment obscured by her cloak. Her appearance suggests a composite of seventeenth and eighteenth century clothing elements for an "old" look, which, along with the broom and high-crowned pointed hat, must have become the identifiers of a witch (plates 3 & 4).

It is likely that what was most recognizable was her lower class condition, in conjunction with her recently-emerged (from where?) hat, and the forever-present broom. In the seventeenth century the stereotype of, or emphasis on, witches being from the lower social class implied certain garment types: coat, wescote and/or bodys over shift, cap and hat, and—infrequently—a cloak. Red was the more prevalent color. Black was also favored, as it was also for Satan. In a mostly hereditary, fixed-status society in which one dressed according to rank, that rank was announced by the garment, not its newness or its relationship to what the elite were wearing. Consequently, since the component garments were sufficient to tag social class, one would not easily confuse an elite woman in silk gown with a launderess in red woollen coat and wescote (*bodys with sleeves*).

By the nineteenth-century, the garment itself was not as much of a distinguishing feature of class as its fashionability and style. A wider range of garment styles became available to the consuming public at every social class level—provided the individual could pay for them. Clothing became more a badge of economic status than of social class position. Therefore, the fashionability of the garment, how new it was within the season, set the social and economic elite apart from the rest. As everyone attempted to participate in this new charade, only the severe antiquity of a garment would tag one as definitely lower class. Perhaps as the elite changed their garment styling more often both in subtle and more overt silhouette variations and the poor held on to their garments longer, that gap between the two extremes on the socio-economic

1. Woodcut of the devil meeting the witch on the highway. Courtesy of the Essex Institute, Salem, MA.

2. The Kingdom of Darkness, 1728. An English woodcut known to have enjoyed wide circulation in New England. Courtesy of the Connecticut Historical Society, Hartford, CT.

3. An early nineteenth-century witch. Reprinted from Pennethorne Hughes,
Witchcraft.

hierarchy widened. Consequently, out-of-style garments became part of
the lower class socio-economic visual stereotyping.

In the 1850s the old hag/crone in pointed hat, riding on a broom
was fully visible in illustrations accompanying the then-popular gothic
and witchcraft novels. Neither these early illustrations nor any story
description of a witch duplicates our modern stereotype of her in black
caftan and/or hooded cloak, or with the pointed hat and broom.

Aside from what now appear to be items inextricably intertwined
with witches—flying brooms, high-crowned pointed hats and black cats—
the women are portrayed as old with long flowing hair, wearing seriously
outmoded fashions. In other words, the hat, broom and cat, in addition
to their age and lowerclass appearance, now depicted through old-
fashioned garments, all mark her a witch. The long flowing dress she
wears is now more reminiscent of the eighteenth-century sack-back gown,
and is closer to the more modern Disney interpretation of a witch in
tunic or flowing caftan. Perhaps one couldn't, or dared not, write about
the witch in true early colonial garments for it is during this time when
the introduction of Thanksgiving pageantry in seventeenth-century dress
first appeared. And Heaven forbid if one should confuse a Pilgrim and
a witch!

4. A witch from a 1856 collection of witchcraft stories. Reprinted from Peter Haining, *A Circle of Witches*.

Although the subject of witches has always been part of the contemporary popular culture, purely fictitious witches do not show up in popular literature until sometime after 1820. Even then, it was enough to label someone a witch, it was not necessary to detail her wicked, unkempt, and old-fashioned appearance. For example, Nathaniel Hawthorne set some of his stories in colonial New England. Yet those which touch on witchcraft do not describe the witches beyond stating they *were* witches, and had a broom or stick to fly to Sabbat on. Hawthorne would have been relying on the strength of the nineteenth-century stereotype of a witch to provide the visual imagery.

It is easy to assume that Halloween costuming of witches helped to solidify the stereotypic witch. Possibly, since Halloween costuming was for children it also marked the transition of witches from adult literature to the children's world of fantasy. Clearly the witch we conjure today is either the Halloween witch or the Walt Disney witch—both of whom belong to children (plates 5 & 6).

It is not clear when Halloween became a nationally celebrated holiday, or when the celebration first included costume. However, it would have been sometime after the 1840s, as the American celebration of Halloween rests on Scottish and Irish folk customs and dates from the immigration of these people. Yet characters in short stories as late as the early 1880s are not always aware of Halloween. Halloween parties and costumes appear in women's magazines in 1903-1904. However, since these same magazines started publication in that year it may be purely coincidental. Even so, costumes were not restricted to those depicting witches and druidic characters, as hobos, for example, were also popular.

IV

During the 1890s, perhaps sparked by the continuing interest in our colonial history, the witch-figure again received attention. That attention came in several forms: use of the stereotype in graphic imagery (plate 5) (which took full advantage of the stereotype); renewed interest in seventeenth-century New England witches, particularly with the anniversary of the Salem witch trials in 1892, and their more human portrayal (plate 7 & 8); and, development of the wicked witch/good witch characters in children's literature (plates 6, 8 & 9).

The 1890 sketch of a Salem witch by R. Norcott reflects historical accuracy in that one of the confined alleged witches in 1692 *did* smoke tobacco. It also continues the imagery of the old and lower class woman as a witch in that she is wearing out-of-fashion, unkempt, plain, woollen garments which would have been worn by an individual of the lower social class—in the late-nineteenth century.

5. Panorama over Salem, 1895. Advertisement for Witch's Cream. Oil painting.
Courtesy of the Essex Institute, Salem, MA.

6. A Walt Disney witch from *Snow White and the Seven Dwarves.*

Pauline Mackie's *Ye Lyttle Salem Maide* in 1901 and the wicked witch in L. Frank Baum's *The Wizard of Oz* (1900), illustrated by W.W. Denslow, demonstrate two different tendencies in our portrayal of witches. Mackie humanizes the seventeenth-century witch, while simultaneously emasculating her in the nineteenth-century tradition. Consequently, while she is dressed in a late-nineteenth-century idea of lower status "colonial" dress she is also an object of pity and ridicule, not the formidable adversary of earlier times. In his *Oz* series Baum separates the witch figure into wicked and good, and they become protagonists in a fairy tale in which good triumphs over evil. These two witches are opposites of each other, as black and white, yet only the details of the "good" witch are ever spelled out in the text. According to Baum, little readers skip descriptive passages because they do not understand them. In this case, the near-universal image of a wicked witch would have made it redundant to describe her. Even so, the illustrations accompanying *The Wizard of Oz* and the popularity of the movie version have probably contributed greatly to our collective memory.

W.W. Denslow, illustrator of the first edition of *The Wizard of Oz*, dressed the good witch similarly to the much earlier woodcut (plate 1 & 8). Perhaps he had the benefit of having seen the earlier depiction during the anniversary of the trials in 1892. In any case, she retained

7. From *Ye Lyttle Salem Maide* by Pauline Mackie, 1901.

8. From *The Wizard of Oz* by L. Frank Baum, illustration by W.W. Denslow, 1900.

9. From *The New Wizard of Oz* by L. Frank Baum, illustration by Evelyn Copeland, 1944.

her high-crowned, pointed hat, as did the munchkins illustrated alongside her.

The illustrator of the 1944 edition of *The New Wizard of Oz*, Evelyn Copeland, appears to meld historical fact with current stereotype. In dressing the wicked witch in red coat and black skirt (plate 9) she may be following the testimony from 1692, yet ascribing 1944 definitions to the terminology. However, Copeland leaves intact the hat and old age imagery of the wicked witch which developed after the New England outbreak.

During the tercentenary of Salem in 1930 the image of a witch, virtually identical to that in the Witch's Cream ad of 1895 and our "Halloween" witch, solidified as a black silhouette of a woman astride a flying broom with long flowing hair, pointed hat and long caftan, and either with or without black cat. Interestingly, sometime before this the witch's broom changed its flying position from handle aft to handle fore.

The legal documents from 1692 were compiled and transcribed in 1938 by the Works Progress Administration, but were not edited and published until 1977. Arthur Miller obviously consulted them while writing his play *The Crucible* (1953) which, while thinly guised as the McCarthy "witch hunt" of the time, takes its story line directly from the factual story of Salem 1692. Aside from the high-crowned hats and great coats worn by the magistrates, no mention is made about dress, nor are any indications of costuming included in the author's notes. Again, we all rely on a commonly-held mental image to lead us through the story and help us separate the witches from the righteous.

Disney dared to get rid of the pointed hat, replacing it by that secondary symbol—the calla, or hooded cloak—, and the broom, while keeping the witch's socio-economic and marital status, and old age. In the seventeenth century the witch had been powerful, feared and considered a formidable adversary. By the nineteenth century she had become an old hag, ugly and eccentric, who lived isolated from her community. In many instances she was more the victim than the powerful maleficent, almost always a symbol of weakness and a target for tricks played by others. Sometime during that century her lower-class status became less important than her pathetic physical appearance and old age. Thus, Disney was able to remove her broom and hat, allow her to hide inside her cloak, and have her offer poisoned apples to beautiful young ladies, all the while knowing that beauty and youth and goodness would win out. The ugly, old, mean witch would in turn die by the end of the tale. Perhaps in so doing, Disney forever split the good and the bad witch, while embuing both with the seventeenth century witch's power and assertiveness.

Later collections of witch stories have illustrations which either reinforce our image of a malefic witch wearing a high-crowned, pointed hat, and long flowing black caftan and cloak, or hooded cloak, following the dual traditions established by Baum and Disney. What was initially a unified image of a powerful and wicked witch split into two as she lost power and was relegated to children's popular culture. Both sets of attire can be seen worn by children at Halloween. They both appear to convey identical symbolism.

V

The high-crowned pointed hat in particular, coupled with knowledge of witchcraft trials and hangings in Salem in 1692, suggests that our modern-day stereotype of a witch might date back to the late-seventeenth century—or earlier. Yet, despite almost striking similarities, the facts reveal that this is not the case. Furthermore, there is virtually nothing written down concerning the details of appearance of a witch. Our mental image of her has always been part of our cultural baggage as part of our collective past experience.

"Witch" is a visual experience. At the utterance of the word we conjure an image. Although that image has changed over time, it still remains strikingly similar and definitely recognizable across time. There is consistency from one decade or century to another attesting to the strength and pervasiveness of the stereotype. A witch is firstly a lower-class female with deformities that come with her advanced age. Her broom, pointed hat or calla signal her bewitching capabilities, while the remainder of her weeds changes to reflect the current stereotype of a lower class person. Today the witch is for children, and Halloween. We accept both the nineteenth-century and the Disney costume versions of a witch. We assume both to be malefic, yet with full knowledge that they are ultimately impotent in the face of their adversaries.

Works Cited

Boyer, Paul and Stephen Nissenbaum. (eds.) *The Salem Witchcraft Papers. Verbatim Transcripts of the Legal Documents of the Salem Witchcraft Outbreak of 1692.* 3 vols. NY: DaCapa Press, 1977.

Demos, John Putnam. *Entertaining Satan: Witchcraft & the Culture of Early New England.* NY: Oxford University Press, 1983.

Hearns, Michael Patrick (ed.) *The Wizard of Oz.* NY:Schocken Books, 1983.

Heyrman, Christine Leigh. *Commerce and Culture. The Maritime Communities of Colonial Massachusetts, 1690-1750.* NY: W.W. Norton, 1984.

Hughes, Pennethorne. *Witchcraft.* Baltimore: Penguin Books, 1965.

Jong, Erica. *Witches.* NY: The New American Library Inc., 1982.

Karlsen, Carol F. *The Devil in the Shape of a Woman. Witchcraft in Colonial New England.* NY: W.W. Norton & Co. 1987.

Linton, Ralph & Adelin. *Halloween through 20 Centuries*. NY: Henry Schuman, 1950.

Mather, Cotton. *Wonders of the Invisible World. Being an Account of the Tryals of Several Witches Lately Executed in New-England*. London: John Russell Smith, 1862. Microfilm edition, University Microfilms, 1972 facsimile copy.

Trautman, Patricia. "When Gentlemen Wore Lace: Sumptuary Legislation and Dress in 17th Century New England," *Journal of Regional Cultures* 2:3, 1983, 9-21.

———. "Dress in Seventeenth-century Cambridge, MA: An Inventory-based Reconstruction," in *Early American Probate Inventories Annual Proceeding* of The Dublin Seminar for New England Folklife, July 11 & 12, 1987, Vol. XII, pp. 51-74. (Boston: Boston University, 1989).

Weisman, Richard. *Witchcraft, Magic and Religion in 17th-century Massachusetts*. Amherst, MA: The University of Massachusetts Press, 1984.

Witches' League for Public Awareness, *Bi-annual Newsletter*, Salem, MA: Witches' League for Public Awareness, P.O. Box 8736, 01971-8736.

Contributors

Patricia A. Cunningham is Associate Professor in the Department of Applied Human Ecology at Bowling Green State University where she teaches such courses as Dress in American Culture, American Material Culture and Twentieth-Century Fashion, as well as Introduction to Women's Studies. She has been a frequent contributor to *Dress, The Journal of the Costume Society of America* and serves on the National Board of that Society. Her current research focuses on "artistic" dress and dress reform.

Susan J. Dickey received a B.A. in history from Texas Lutheran College in 1977 and two years later earned an M.A. in museum studies from Texas Tech University. In 1984, as Curator of Costumes at the Indiana State Museum, she organized the "25 Years of Barbie Dolls" exhibition. She is currently working toward a Ph.D. in history at Texas Tech.

Beverly Gordon is Associate Professor in the Department of Environment, Textiles and Design at the University of Wisconsin-Madison. She also serves as Director of the Helen Allen Textile Collection at the University, and is affiliated with the Women's Studies Program. Her interests lie in the aspects of material culture that are most intimate and personal: dress, small handmade objects, and the home environment.

Lillian O. Holloman is Assistant Professor in the Department of Microenvironmental Studies and Design at Howard University. Both her M.S. (from the University of Illinois, Champaign-Urbana) and her Ph.D. (from Michigan State University) are in clothing and textiles. Dr. Holloman has published books and articles in both academic and popular literatue and is an active member of several professional organizations, including The Association of College Professors of Textiles and Clothing (ACPTC). The Costume Society of America and the Society for Human Ecology.

Susan Voso Lab is an Assistant Professor in the Department of Applied Human Ecology at Bowling Green State University where she teaches Historic Costumes and Textile Collections Management and History of Costume, as well as advanced design courses. Her current activities include work with several university and community historic collections, editing two books and researching pre-Columbian Peruvian textiles as well as other material culture artifacts.

Albert LeBlanc is an active researcher in the field of music preference and has proposed a formal theory to explain the development of individual music listening preferences. He became interested in popular music through his research, and has developed a sequence of courses for nonmusic majors examining the history of American popular music in the twentieth century. LeBlanc is a former chairman of the Society for Research in Music Education of Music Educators National Conference and is Professor of Music at Michigan State University.

Barbara K. Nordquist is Professor in the Department of Microenvironmental Studies and Design at Howard University. Her teenage children, although not punks themselves, introduced her to the phenomenon. Her current research interests are in folk textiles and dress and African American dress and adornment.

Alexandra Palmer is a Ph.D. candidate at Brighton Polytechnic, U.K. in the Department of Art and Design History. She received her MA in Costume and Textile History from New York University (1981).

Kathleen L. Rowold received a Ph.D. in apparel and textile history from Purdue University before joining the faculty at Indiana University, Bloomington, Indiana. Professor Rowold serves as chairperson of the Department of Apparel Merchandising and Interior Design and teaches costume history and the behavioral aspects of dress. Her current research is related to her activities as Curator of the Sage Costume Collection at Indiana University.

Pamela J. Schlick received an M.S. in History of Costume and an M.S. in Instructional Systems Technology, both from Indiana University. As former Assistant Curator of the Sage Costume Collection at Indiana University, she conducted research in systematic methods of classifying and dating historic costume. Currently, Ms. Schlick is a Systems Designer with Applied Science Associates, Somerset, New Jersey.

Sally Sims is the Curator of the National Trust for Historic Preservation Library Collection of the University of Maryland, College Park. She holds a B.A. from the College of William and Mary; an M.L.S. from Clarion University of Pennsylvania; and an M.A. in American Studies from the George Washington University, where she was a National Endowment for the Humanities Fellow. This essay is based on her 1975 M.A. thesis, *The Bicycle, the Bloomer, and the "New Woman": Images of the American Woman Awheel, 1890-1899.*

Pat Trautman teaches material culture of the family in the School of Family Studies at the University of Connecticut. She specializes in the study of American dress as a reflection of its social setting. She is currently editor of *Dress, The Journal of The Costume Society of America.*